Wonderful ways to prepare

# FISH & SEAFOOD

by MARION MANSFIELD

SCALLOPS IN SAFFRON SAUCE (RECIPE PAGE 21)

Wonderful ways to prepare

# FISH & SEAFOOD

H.C. PUBLISHING INC.
FLORIDA, USA

COVER PICTURE—SEAFOOD SALAD WITH HERB VINAIGRETTE (RECIPE PAGE 21)

FIRST PUBLISHED 1979
REPRINTED 1984
FIRST US EDITION 1984

PUBLISHED AND COPYRIGHT © 1979
BY AYERS & JAMES
CROWS NEST, N.S.W., AUSTRALIA

DISTRIBUTED BY
AYERS & JAMES, CROWS NEST, N.S.W., AUSTRALIA
H.C. PUBLISHING INC., U.S.A.

PRINTED IN SINGAPORE

HARD COVER EDITION: ISBN 0 87637 922 6
SOFT COVER EDITION: ISBN 0 87637 934 X

TITLES AVAILABLE IN THIS SERIES: BEEF,
FISH & SEAFOOD, POULTRY, STEWS & CASSEROLES,
BARBECUES & PICNIC MEALS, CHINESE MEALS,
SALADS, SOUPS, ITALIAN MEALS, LAMB,
CAKES & COOKIES, DESSERTS.

◄ OVERLEAF—FRIED SOLE WITH PARSLEY MAYONNAISE (RECIPE PAGE 20)          PRAWNS & BACON (RECIPE PAGE 20) ►

# Scallops in Garlic Cream Sauce

Melt butter in a pan, add garlic, parsley, wine, salt and pepper. Cover and simmer for 15 minutes, add scallops and simmer 5 minutes. Uncover and stir in cream, heat but do not boil. Serve immediately.

Serves: 4
Cooking time: 25 minutes

   1½ lbs (750 g) scallops
   3 tablespoons butter
   2 cloves garlic, crushed
   3 tablespoons chopped parsley
   salt and pepper
   ¼ cup (65 ml) cream

# Whiting with Vegetables

Serves:   4
Cooking time:   30 minutes

    4 small whole whiting, cleaned
    salt and pepper
    4 tablespoons flour
    1½ tablespoons curry powder
    oil for frying
    2 small squash, sliced lengthways
    2 small eggplants, sliced lengthways
    1 lemon, sliced in rings
    parsley

Sprinkle fish with salt. Mix flour and curry powder together and dust fish liberally. Heat oil in a pan, add fish and cook until golden on all sides. Remove fish to a serving dish and keep warm. Sprinkle squash and eggplant with salt and pepper, add to the pan juices and sauté until golden brown. Remove to the serving dish and garnish with lemon rings and parsley.

# Trout, Mushrooms and Leeks

Serves: 4
Cooking time: 45–50 minutes

*4 trout*
*salt*
*1 clove garlic, crushed*
*3 tablespoons chopped parsley*
*juice of 1 lemon*
*½ cup (125 ml) white wine*
*3 tablespoons butter*
*10–12 leek bulbs*
*½ lb (250 g) button mushrooms, sliced*
*1 tablespoon flour*
*salt and pepper*
*½ cup (125 ml) concentrated fish stock—see recipe page 89*

Sprinkle trout inside and out with salt and place in a flameproof casserole dish. Mix garlic, half the parsley, lemon juice and wine and pour over the fish; set fish aside to marinate for 1 hour. Drain off marinade and reserve.

Melt half the butter in a pan, add leeks and mushrooms and sauté for 5–6 minutes to lightly brown leeks; remove leeks and mushrooms and replace with fish. Add remaining butter to pan juices, stir in flour and cook until bubbly; gradually stir in stock and reserved marinade, bring to the boil, stirring constantly, then pour over the fish. Cover tightly and simmer gently for 25–30 minutes.

Serve trout, mushrooms and leeks sprinkled with remaining parsley.

# Spanish Herrings

Serves: 4
Cooking time: 45–50 minutes
Oven: 160°C 325°F

4 herrings, sardines or small mullet
salt and pepper
1½ tablespoons lemon juice
4 tablespoons oil
2 large onions, chopped
1 clove garlic, crushed
1 lb (500 g) tomatoes, peeled and chopped
1 red bell pepper, seeded and chopped
½ teaspoon oregano
salt and dash of seasoned pepper
1½ tablespoons chopped parsley
½ cup (125 ml) white wine
¾ cup (185 ml) hot water

Place fish in an ovenproof casserole dish and sprinkle with salt, pepper and lemon juice. Heat oil in a pan, add onions and garlic and sauté until soft, add tomatoes and red bell pepper and cook, stirring, 4–5 minutes. Stir in oregano, salt, seasoned pepper, parsley, wine and hot water. Bring to the boil and cook gently for 5 minutes. Pour mixture over the fish, cover and cook in a moderately slow oven for 30 minutes. Serve hot with rice or noodles.

# Shrimp on Rice

Serves: 4
Cooking time: 15–20 minutes

*1½ lbs (750 g) cooked shrimp*
*3 tablespoons butter*
*salt and seasoned pepper*
*2 tablespoons chopped parsley*
*juice of 1 lemon*
*½ cup (125 ml) white wine*
*hot boiled rice*

Reserve 6 shrimp for garnish. Shell and de-vein the remainder. Melt butter in a pan, add shelled shrimp and stir to lightly coat with the butter. Season with salt and pepper, add parsley, sprinkle lemon juice over and stir in wine. Cover and simmer gently for 15 minutes.
Serve over hot rice, garnished with the 6 shrimp.

BAKED CLAMS (RECIPE PAGE 12) ▶

# Tuna Tart

Serves:   4
Cooking time:   20–25 minutes
Oven:   180°C   350°F

15¾ oz (450 g) can tuna, drained
1 pastry shell
2 tablespoons butter
1 medium onion, minced
salt and pepper
1 teaspoon thyme
4 tablespoons tomato paste
½ cup tomato purée
15–20 black olives, pitted

Melt butter in a pan, add onion and sauté 1–2 minutes, add salt, pepper and thyme, stir in tomato paste and purée and heat, stirring constantly. Place tuna pieces in the pastry shell and pour mixture over. Top with black olives. Cook in a moderate oven for 15 minutes.
Serve hot or cold.

# Baked Clams

Serves:   4
Cooking time:   15 minutes
Oven:   180°C   350°F

48 clams on the shell
3 tablespoons chopped parsley
4 anchovies, finely chopped
2 cloves garlic, crushed
2 teaspoons oregano
2 tablespoons oil
salt and pepper
1 cup (250 ml) white wine
(oysters may be used in place of clams)

Arrange clam shells on an oven tray. In a bowl combine parsley, anchovies, garlic, oregano, oil, salt, pepper and wine and mix well. Spoon mixture over clams and cook in a pre-heated moderate oven for 15 minutes.
Serve immediately.
(Illustrated on page 11.)

# Mackerel with Cream and Parsley

Serves:   4
Cooking time:   20 minutes

  4 mackerel, boned
  ½ cup (125 ml) salad oil
  ¼ cup (65 ml) lemon juice
  2 cloves garlic, crushed
  2 tablespoons chopped parsley
  ½ cup dry breadcrumbs
  ¼ cup grated cheese
  ¼ teaspoon salt
  dash seasoned pepper
  2 tablespoons butter
  ½ cup (125 ml) heavy cream

Combine salad oil, lemon juice, half the crushed garlic and half the parsley and mix well to a sauce. Mix breadcrumbs, cheese, remaining garlic, salt and seasoned pepper for coating. Heat butter in a pan. Dip fish in sauce, then into coating and place in the pan. Cook slowly, turning often and basting with the sauce, for about 15 minutes; fish should become flaky. Pour the cream over the fish and sprinkle with remaining parsley.

# Whiting and Tomatoes with Noodles

Serves: 4
Cooking time: 45 minutes
Oven: 180°C 350°F

1½ lbs (750 g) fillets of whiting
salt and pepper
dash of thyme
1 cup (250 ml) white wine
3 tablespoons butter
3 medium onions, sliced
¾ lb (375 g) tomatoes, cut in wedges
½ lb (250 g) champignons, sliced
2 tablespoons grated cheese
½ teaspoon seasoned pepper
hot noodles

Place fish fillets in a greased ovenproof casserole dish, season with salt, pepper and thyme and pour wine over. Cover and cook gently for 10 minutes. Meanwhile, melt butter in a pan, add onions and sauté until transparent, add tomatoes and mushrooms and cook, stirring, for 5 minutes. Stir in cheese and seasoned pepper and cook a further 3–4 minutes. Spoon mixture on top of fish and cook, uncovered, in a moderate oven for 15–20 minutes. Serve with hot noodles.

PASTRY WRAPPED FISH (RECIPE PAGE 17) ▶

SMOKED HADDOCK IN CREAM SAUCE (RECIPE OPPOSITE PAGE)

SEAFOOD IN CREAM SAUCE (RECIPE OPPOSITE PAGE)

# Smoked Haddock in Cream Sauce

Serves:  4
Cooking time:   20–25 minutes

1½ lbs (750 g) — 4 pieces smoked haddock
7¾ oz (220 g) can button mushrooms, drained
1 cup (250 ml) milk
dash of seasoned pepper
½ teaspoon grated nutmeg
1½ tablespoons flour
½ cup (125 ml) heavy cream


In a large pan place the haddock, cover with water, bring to a boil and drain. Add champignons, milk, pepper and nutmeg, 12 oz. Cover and simmer gently for 15 minutes. Carefully remove fish and keep hot. Blend the flour with a little of the milk and add this to the liquid. Stir until boiling; remove from heat and fold in the cream. Heat but do not boil. Pour cream sauce over fish at serving.
*(Illustrated on opposite page.)*


# Seafood in Cream Sauce

Serves:   4–6
Cooking time:   15–20 minutes

½ lb (250 g) scallops
24 mussels
½ lb (250 g) shrimp
½ lb (250 g) fish fillets, cut in small pieces
5 tablespoons butter
1½ tablespoons flour
salt and pepper
1 cup (250 ml) heavy cream
cooked rice


Scrub mussels under running water and steam in a pan with 1 cup water for 5–6 minutes to open; remove the shells and beards.
Melt butter in a pan, add scallops, mussels, shrimp and fish and cook for 4–5 minutes; sprinkle with flour, salt and pepper and cook gently, stirring for 4–5 minutes. Fold in cream and cook, stirring constantly, until sauce is smooth. Serve with cooked rice.
*(Illustrated on opposite page.)*


# Pastry Wrapped Fish

Serves:   4–6
Cooking time:   45–50 minutes
Oven:   200°C   400°F

1 lb (500 g) fish fillets
¼ cup (65 ml) white wine
5 tablespoons butter
1 medium onion, chopped finely
2 scallions, chopped finely
¼ lb (125 g) mushrooms, sliced
2 teaspoons saffron
1 cup cooked rice
2 hard boiled eggs, chopped
¼ lb (125 g) fish roe (optional)
12 oz (375 g) packet frozen puff pastry, thawed
1 egg, beaten with a little water
watercress


In a pan lightly poach fish fillets in wine for 5 minutes, drain fish, flake and set aside, reserve the liquid.
Melt 1 tablespoon of butter in a pan, add onion and scallions and sauté until transparent; remove and set aside. Add 1 tablespoon of butter to pan juices, add mushrooms and cook gently for 5 minutes, remove and set aside. Melt remaining 2 tablespoons of butter in a pan, stir in saffron and rice, heat and stir to coat rice with saffron butter, remove from heat and set aside.
Grease a glass or plastic loaf pan; place half the saffron rice in the base in a layer, cover with a layer of half the onion and scallions, then add half the mushrooms, then half the hard boiled eggs. Spread all the fish in a layer, place roe down the center of the fish. Cover the fish in order with layers of remaining eggs, mushrooms, onion and scallions, and lastly the saffron rice. Pour reserved liquid over the top. Refrigerate for at least 3 hours.
Roll out pastry to ½″ (1 cm) thickness, turn out terrine carefully into center and wrap pastry around; press edges firmly together; do not overlap pastry too thickly. Place in a greased baking dish, brush with beaten egg and cook in a hot oven for 20–25 minutes until golden brown. Serve pastry wrapped fish sliced thickly, garnished with watercress.
*(Illustrated on page 15.)*

# Sole in Sherry

Serves:  4
Cooking time:  20 minutes
Oven:  190°C  375°F

1½ lbs (750 g) fillets of sole
4 tablespoons butter
salt and seasoned pepper
¾ cup (185 ml) sherry
parsley butter — see recipe page 92

Arrange skinned and boned sole fillets in a well buttered ovenproof casserole dish, sprinkle fish with salt and seasoned pepper; pour wine over the fish and dot with remaining butter, cover and cook in a moderately hot oven for 20 minutes.
Serve sole with wine butter sauce and top with pats of parsley butter.

FISH STEAKS WITH CREAMY CHEESE SAUCE (RECIPE PAGE 21) ▶

# Prawns and Bacon

Serves: 4
Cooking time: 25–30 minutes

1 lb (500 g) prawns or shrimp, shelled and
   de-veined
½ lb (250 g) bacon, chopped
2 tablespoons oil
2 scallions, finely chopped
1 clove garlic, crushed
1 tablespoon chopped parsley
2 tablespoons soy sauce
¾ cup (185 ml) white wine
4 tablespoons butter
1 medium onion, chopped
1 teaspoon thyme
½ teaspoon sage
salt and pepper
1 cup soft breadcrumbs
4 eggs beaten

Cook bacon in pan lightly, remove, keep warm.
Add prawns to the pan juices, sauté until heated
through. Remove and place with the bacon. To pan
juices add oil and heat, add scallions, garlic and
parsley and cook 1–2 minutes, stir in soy sauce
and wine, bring to the boil, cover and simmer for 10
minutes.
Meanwhile melt butter in a pan, add onion and
sauté until transparent, add thyme, sage, salt,
pepper and soft breadcrumbs and cook, stirring
constantly, for 3 minutes, fold in beaten eggs and
cook, still stirring, for 3 minutes.
Serve bread mixture in the center of a dish and ring
with the prawns, pour wine sauce over and top with
bacon.
(Illustrated on page 5.)

# Fried Oysters with Fried Parsley

Serves: 4
Cooking time: 15–20 minutes

24 oysters for 4 persons
flour
salt and pepper
1 egg, beaten with a little water
dry breadcrumbs
oil for frying
fried parsley
hot tartare sauce — see recipe page 90

Dredge oysters in flour seasoned with salt and
pepper, dip in beaten egg and toss in breadcrumbs. Heat oil in a deep pan, add oysters in a
cooking basket and cook until golden, drain on
kitchen paper and keep hot.
Fried parsley: Wash sprigs of parsley, dry well.
Refrigerate for 30 minutes, then place parsley in a
basket. Heat oil in a deep pan and carefully lower
basket into hot oil; it will spit and sizzle. When
sizzling stops, remove and drain parsley on paper
towels.
Serve fried oysters and fried parsley with hot
tartare sauce.

# Fried Sole with Parsley Mayonnaise

Serves: 4
Cooking time: 15–20 minutes

1½ lbs (750 g) fillets of sole
juice of 1 lemon
1 cup mayonnaise
2 tablespoons chopped parsley
¾ cup (185 ml) milk
3 tablespoons flour
oil for frying
lemon wedges
lettuce leaves for garnish

Slice fillets of sole into strips and place in a shallow
glass dish, sprinkle lemon juice over and let stand
for 15 minutes. Mix mayonnaise and parsley
together until smooth, and chill. Blend milk and
flour together to a smooth batter and coat fish
strips.
Heat oil in a pan until hot, add fish and cook on all
sides until golden brown; drain on paper towels.
Serve fish with parsley mayonnaise, garnished with
lemon wedges and lettuce leaves.
(Illustrated on pages 2 and 3.)

# Scallops in Saffron Sauce

Serves:  4
Cooking time:  20 minutes

*1 lb (500 g) scallops*
*1 cup (250 ml) white wine*
*2 scallions, finely chopped*
*juice of 1 lemon*
*1½ tablespoons butter*
*1½ tablespoons flour*
*salt and pepper*
*1 teaspoon saffron*
*½ cup (125 ml) heavy cream*
*shrimp as garnish (optional)*

Wash and dry scallops and place in a pan with wine, scallions and lemon juice and bring to the boil, reduce heat, cover and simmer for 5–6 minutes. Strain off liquid and reserve; keep scallops and scallions hot.
Melt butter in a pan, add flour, salt, pepper and saffron and cook 1–2 minutes, gradually stir in reserved liquid and bring to the boil, stirring constantly. Remove from heat and fold in cream. Heat, but do not boil.
Serve saffron sauce over scallions and garnish with a few prawns.
*(Illustrated on page 1.)*

# Fish Steaks with Creamy Cheese Sauce

Serves:  4
Cooking time:  35–40 minutes

*4 fish steaks*
*4 tablespoons butter*
*1 cup (250 ml) dry white wine*
*¼ lb (125 g) mushrooms, finely sliced*
*1½ tablespoons flour*
*¼ cup grated cheese*
*salt and pepper*
*½ cup (125 ml) cream*
*cooked crisp bacon pieces*

Melt 1 tablespoon butter in a pan, add fish steaks and cook 2 minutes on each side, pour wine over fish, cover and simmer for 10 minutes. Strain off liquid and reserve. Keep fish hot.

Melt 1 tablespoon butter in the pan, add mushrooms and sauté for 4–5 minutes; remove mushrooms and place with the fish. Add remaining butter to the pan, stir in flour, cheese, salt and pepper and cook, stirring, 1–2 minutes. Gradually stir in reserved liquid and heat, stirring constantly, until sauce thickens. Fold in cream and heat, but do not boil.
Serve fish steaks and mushrooms with creamy cheese sauce.
*(Illustrated on page 19.)*

# Seafood Salad with Herb Vinaigrette

Serves:  4
No cooking

*½ lb (250 g) cooked shrimp, shelled and*
    *de-veined*
*½ lb (250 g) cooked mussels*
*4–6 oysters*
*2 stalks celery, chopped*
*celery leaves*
*1 medium carrot, shredded*
*1 medium white onion, thinly sliced*
*1 cup shredded cabbage*
*3 lettuce leaves, torn*

**Herb Vinaigrette:**
*½ teaspoon dry mustard*
*pinch salt*
*dash seasoned pepper*
*3 tablespoons wine vinegar*
*1 teaspoon chopped parsley*
*1 teaspoon tarragon*
*1 teaspoon chopped chives*
*1 ice cube*
*8 tablespoons salad oil*

To make herb vinaigrette: In a jar mix mustard and salt with a little vinegar until smooth, add parsley, tarragon and chives and stir in the remainder of the vinegar, cover and shake briskly. Add ice cube, then oil, a few drops at a time, stirring. Cover and shake briskly. Refrigerate at least 1 hour.
In a salad bowl place chilled celery and leaves, carrot, onion, cabbage and lettuce and toss. Place shrimp, mussels and oysters on top, shake and sprinkle herb vinaigrette over.
*(Illustrated on front cover and page 4.)*

# Seasoned Fish Rolls

Serves: 4
Cooking time: 15 minutes

*1½ lbs (750 g) — 4 fillets of sole*
*1 tablespoon chopped parsley*
*3 anchovy fillets, finely chopped (optional)*
*1 tablespoon capers, chopped*
*2 small pickled cucumbers, finely chopped*
*2 eggs*
*½ cup soft breadcrumbs*
*dry breadcrumbs*
*1 tablespoon grated cheese*
*½ teaspoon salt*
*flour*
*oil for frying*
*rock melon balls (optional)*
*extra chopped parsley*

Skin and bone the fish fillets. Combine parsley, anchovies, capers, cucumbers, 1 egg and soft breadcrumbs and mix together for seasoning, spoon onto fish fillets, roll up and fasten with a toothpick. Beat remaining egg with a little water. Mix dry breadcrumbs, cheese and salt together. Dredge fish rolls with flour, dip in egg and toss in cheese breadcrumbs to coat. Heat oil in a pan, add fish rolls and cook until golden brown all over. Serve seasoned fish rolls with rock melon balls and sprinkle with parsley.

BREADED SARDINES (RECIPE PAGE 24)

BAKED FISH WITH STEAMED RICE (RECIPE PAGE 24)

# Breaded Sardines

Serves: 4
Cooking time: 35–40 minutes
Oven: 180°C 350°F

1½ lbs (750 g) filleted sardines
1½ tablespoons oil
salt and pepper
1 tablespoon lemon juice
1 medium onion, finely sliced
1 tablespoon chopped parsley
dry breadcrumbs
1½ tablespoons butter
½ cup (125 ml) concentrated fish stock — see
   recipe page 89
½ cup (125 ml) white wine

Arrange sardines in a greased ovenproof casserole dish, brush with oil and sprinkle with salt, pepper and lemon juice. Arrange onion sliced on top, spread with parsley and dry breadcrumbs and dot with butter. Pour the stock and wine over the fish and cover. Cook in a moderate oven for 15 minutes. Remove cover and cook a further 15–20 minutes until golden brown.
(Illustrated on page 23.)

# Baked Fish with Steamed Rice

Serves: 4
Cooking time: 40–45 minutes
Oven: 190°C 375°F

8 small fresh fish
3 tablespoons oil
1½ lbs (750 g) tomatoes, peeled, chopped
1 clove garlic, crushed
1 teaspoon thyme
1 bay leaf
salt and pepper
1 lemon, sliced in rings
8 oz (237 g) bottle of black olives

### Steamed Rice:
1 cup rice
1 teaspoon salt
2½ cups (625 ml) boiling water
4 tablespoons butter
1 egg, beaten
1 teaspoon seasoned pepper
1 teaspoon thyme

Heat oil in a pan, add tomatoes, garlic, thyme, bay leaf, salt and pepper and cook, stirring for 5–6 minutes; cover and simmer sauce for 5 minutes; discard bay leaf. Clean fish and place in a greased ovenproof casserole dish. Arrange lemon slices on top, spoon sauce over the fish and add black olives. Cover and cook in a moderately hot oven for 20–25 minutes.
Meanwhile for the rice: place rice in a greased ovenproof casserole dish, sprinkle with salt and pour over the boiling water. Cover and cook in a moderately hot oven for 20–25 minutes. Remove from oven and stir in butter, egg, seasoned pepper and thyme.
Serve baked fish with the steamed rice.
(Illustrated on page 23.)

# Baked Seasoned Snapper

Serves: 4
Cooking time: 40 minutes
Oven: 200°C 400°F

2 lbs (1 kg) whole snapper
4 tablespoons butter
1 medium onion, finely chopped
1 small bell pepper, seeded and finely chopped
1 tablespoon chopped parsley
salt and pepper
1 teaspoon mixed herbs
1 cup soft breadcrumbs
½ cup (125 ml) white wine

Melt 1 tablespoon of butter in a pan, add onion and bell pepper and sauté until soft. Remove from pan into a bowl and combine with parsley, salt, pepper, herbs, breadcrumbs and wine to make the seasoning.
Dust the fish inside and out with salt and pepper, fill cavity with seasoning, pressing lightly, and close with skewers. Lay fish on buttered foil and dot with remaining butter, wrap fish to seal and place in a baking dish. Cook in a hot oven for 25 minutes, uncover fish and cook a further 10 minutes.

# Baked Trout in Wine

Serves: 4
Cooking time: 20–25 minutes
Oven: 200°C 400°F

2 lbs (1 kg) — 4 small trout, cleaned
2 tablespoons lemon juice
salt and pepper
3 cloves garlic, crushed
1 cup (250 ml) white wine
4 scallions, finely chopped
2 tablespoons chopped parsley
2 tablespoons dry breadcrumbs
4 tablespoons butter, melted

Brush trout inside and out with lemon juice and season with salt and pepper. Spread crushed garlic over base of a greased ovenproof casserole dish. Arrange fish on garlic and pour wine over fish, top with scallions, parsley and breadcrumbs and spread melted butter on top. Cook, uncovered, in a hot oven for 20 minutes until top is golden brown.

# Baked Seasoned Bream

Serves: 4
Cooking time: 30 minutes
Oven: 180°C 350°F

2 lbs (1 kg) — 4 bream
8 tablespoons butter
1 large onion, finely chopped
1 clove garlic, crushed
¼ lb (125 g) mushrooms, chopped
dash of basil
dash of chervil
1 tablespoon chopped parsley
salt and pepper
2 hard boiled eggs, chopped
1 tablespoon capers, chopped
1½ cups soft breadcrumbs
1½ cups (375 ml) white wine
extra salt

Clean and bone fish, remove heads, sprinkle cavity with salt and lay them in a foil lined baking dish. Melt 3 tablespoons of butter in a pan, add onion and garlic and sauté lightly until transparent, stir in mushrooms and cook for 2 minutes, add basil, chervil, 1 teaspoon of parsley, salt and pepper and stir. Remove from heat and add eggs, capers, breadcrumbs and 1 tablespoon of melted butter and mix for seasoning. Pack cavity of each fish with a portion of seasoning mixture, fold flesh together. Brush each fish with 1 tablespoon of melted butter and pour wine over, dot with remaining butter. Cover tightly with foil and cook in a moderate oven for 25 minutes. At serving sprinkle with remainder of parsley.

# Fish Fillets in Wine Sauce

Serves: 4
Cooking time: 25–30 minutes
Oven: 180°C 350°F

1½ lbs (750 g) fish fillets
4 tablespoons butter or margarine
1 medium onion, chopped
1½ cups (375 ml) white wine
bouquet garni
salt and pepper
1 tablespoon flour
chopped parsley

Melt 1 tablespoon butter in a pan, add onion and sauté until lightly browned, add wine and bouquet garni and boil to reduce liquid by half; discard bouquet garni. Strain liquid and reserve. Melt remaining butter in a pan, add fish and brown on each side, sprinkle with salt and pepper. Transfer fish to a greased ovenproof casserole. Add flour to pan juices, stir and cook 1–2 minutes, stir in reserved liquid and bring to the boil, stirring constantly. Pour sauce over the fish, cover and cook in a moderate oven for 15 minutes.
Serve with wine sauce, sprinkled with parsley.

# Cod Steaks and Leeks

Serves: 4
Cooking time: 40–45 minutes

*4 cod steaks*
*1½ cups (375 ml) dry white wine*
*1½ cups (375 ml) water*
*2 medium onions, sliced*
*2 cloves*
*salt and pepper*
*½ teaspoon thyme*
*1 bay leaf*
*4 leeks, chopped*
*½ cup (125 ml) cream*
*pinch of nutmeg*

Make court-bouillon by combining wine, water, onions, cloves, salt, pepper, thyme and bay leaf in a pan. Bring to the boil and simmer for 15 minutes. To this liquid add the fish and simmer for 7–8 minutes. Remove cod steaks carefully and keep warm. Boil court-bouillon to reduce to 1 cup. Discard bay leaf. Add leeks and simmer for 6–7 minutes. Fold in cream and nutmeg and heat, but do not boil.

Serve sauce over cod steaks.

26

SCALLOP OMELETTE (RECIPE PAGE 28) ▶

# Scallop Omelette

Serves: 1
Cooking time: 20–25 minutes

*¼ lb (125 g) scallops for each serving*
*1½ tablespoons butter*
*1 clove garlic, crushed*
*salt and pepper*
*2 eggs*
*3 tablespoons water*
*extra butter*

Wash, dry and trim scallops and cut corals. Melt butter in a pan, add garlic and scallops and corals and cook gently, stirring, 3–4 minutes. Break eggs into a bowl, add salt, pepper and water and beat lightly with a fork.

In an omelette pan place a teaspoon of butter, melt and smear base of pan; turn egg mixture into pan and cook over moderate heat, stirring with the point of knife, for 2–3 minutes. Spoon ½ the scallops onto one side of egg mixture and fold omelette over carefully with a spatula or egg slice and cook 1–2 minutes. Place remaining scallops on top of omelette. Transfer pan to the broiler and cook 2″ (5 cm) from heat to lightly brown. Serve immediately. *(Illustrated on page 27.)*

# Bream Baked with Tomatoes

Serves: 4
Cooking time: 30 minutes
Oven: 180°C 350°F

*2 lbs (1 kg) — 4 small bream*
*4 tablespoons butter*
*2 large onions, sliced thinly*
*1 clove garlic, crushed*
*½ cup (125 ml) vermouth or white wine*
*2 large tomatoes, peeled and sliced*
*dash of thyme*
*parsley*
*salt and pepper*

Melt 2 tablespoons of butter in a pan, add onions and sauté until soft, add garlic, stir in vermouth and cook 2–3 minutes.

Arrange fish in a foil lined baking dish, pour onion sauce over and top with tomato slices, salt, pepper, thyme and parsley; dot with the remaining butter, cover tightly with foil and cook in a moderate oven for 25 minutes. Baste once during cooking.

# Bream in Creamy Sauce

Serves: 4
Cooking time: 35–40 minutes
Oven: 180°C 350°F

*1½ lbs (750 g) fillets of bream*
*3 tablespoons butter*
*1 large onion, chopped*
*¼ lb (125 g) button mushrooms, sliced*
*2 tablespoons chopped parsley*
*salt and pepper*
*1 cup (250 ml) white wine*
*1½ tablespoons flour*
*½ cup (125 ml) cream*

Arrange fish fillets in a greased ovenproof casserole dish. Melt 1 tablespoon of butter in a pan, add onion and sauté until transparent, add mushrooms, ½ the parsley, the salt and pepper; gradually stir in the wine. Bring to the boil, stirring, lower heat and simmer for 2–3 minutes and pour over the fish. Cover and cook in a moderate oven for 25 minutes. Drain off liquid and reserve and keep fish hot.

Melt remaining butter in a pan, stir in flour and cook until bubbly, gradually stir in reserved liquid, bring to the boil and simmer 4–5 minutes, stirring constantly. Fold in cream and heat, but do not boil. Serve creamy sauce over bream fillets and sprinkle with remaining parsley.

# Buttered Trout

Serves: 4
Cooking time: 25 minutes

2 lbs (1 kg) — 4 small trout
salt
flour
6 tablespoons butter
½ teaspoon mace
½ teaspoon sage
dash of black pepper
lemon rind and juice
2 tablespoons chopped parsley

Season inside and out of fish with salt and dredge with flour. Melt 3 tablespoons of butter in a pan, add fish and cook, turning often, until golden brown; remove fish and keep warm.

To the pan juices add remaining butter and melt, stir in mace, sage, black pepper, lemon rind and juice and ½ the parsley; simmer, stirring constantly, for 2–3 minutes. Serve sauce over trout and sprinkle with remaining parsley.

# Butter Fried Fish Fillets

Serves: 4
Cooking time: 20 minutes

1½ lbs (750 g) fillets of fish
flour
salt and pepper
6 tablespoons butter
½ cup (125 ml) lemon juice
1 tablespoon chopped parsley

Dredge fish in flour seasoned with salt and pepper. Melt 3 tablespoons of butter in a pan, add fish and cook until golden all over; remove fish and keep hot. Add remainder of butter to pan juices and heat, stir in 1 tablespoon of leftover seasoned flour and cook until bubbly, add parsley and gradually stir in lemon juice; cook until thickened, stirring constantly, and simmer for 3 minutes. Pour sauce over fish and serve.

# Crab Bisque

Serves: 4
Cooking time: 15–20 minutes

15¾ oz (450 g) can crab meat, drained and flaked
4 cups (1 liter) concentrated fish stock — see recipe page 89
4 egg yolks
¾ cup (185 ml) cream
salt and pepper
dash of nutmeg
chopped parsley

Heat fish stock in a deep pan until boiling. Beat egg yolks with cream until smooth and fold into the stock, reduce heat and simmer gently, stirring constantly, until the mixture thickens; season with salt, pepper and nutmeg. Fold in crabmeat and simmer 1–2 minutes and serve sprinkled with parsley.

# Casserole of Fish Fillets

Serves: 4
Cooking time: 35–40 minutes
Oven: 180°C 350°F

1½ lbs (750 g) fillets of fish
1 tablespoon lemon juice
salt and pepper
1 teaspoon paprika
¾ cup (185 ml) white wine
3 tablespoons butter or margarine
1 medium onion, chopped
1 stalk of celery, chopped
1 small bell pepper, seeded and chopped
1 tablespoon chopped parsley.

Place fish in an ovenproof casserole dish and sprinkle with lemon juice, salt, pepper and paprika, add wine, cover and let stand for ½ hour. Drain off liquid and reserve.

Meanwhile, melt butter in a pan, add onion ad sauté until soft, add celery, bell pepper and parsley and braise over moderate heat, stirring occasionally, for 10 minutes. Stir in reserved liquid, then spoon mixture over fish. Cover and cook in a pre-heated moderate oven for 20–25 minutes.

# Scallops Cooked with Ham

Serves:  4–6
Cooking time:  25–30 minutes

1½ lbs (750 g) scallops
scallop shells (optional)
¾ cup (185 ml) white wine
1½ tablespoons butter
2 scallions, chopped finely
¼ lb (125 g) ham, chopped
¼ cup (65 ml) cream
chopped parsley

Wash and dry shells. Dry scallops on paper towels. Heat wine in a pan, add scallops, cover and simmer gently for 4–5 minutes. Remove scallops and set aside, but reserve the liquid. Melt butter in a pan, add scallions and sauté 2–3 minutes, add ham and heat through for 1–2 minutes; season with salt and pepper. Stir in reserved liquid and simmer 4–5 minutes. Return scallops to the pan and stir in cream; heat but do not boil.
Spoon mixture into warm shells or individual dishes and sprinkle with chopped parsley.

SMOKED HADDOCK WITH MUSTARD SAUCE (RECIPE PAGE 32)

WHITING IN CAPER SAUCE (RECIPE PAGE 32)

# Whiting in Caper Sauce

Serves: 4
Cooking time: 20–25 minutes

1½ lbs (750 g) fillets of whiting
salt and pepper
flour
oil for frying

**Sauce:**
1½ tablespoons butter
1½ tablespoons flour
½ teaspoon dry mustard
1 cup (250 ml) white wine
1.teaspoon wine or malt vinegar
2 tablespoons capers
1½ tablespoons heavy cream

Dredge fish fillets with flour seasoned with salt and pepper. Heat oil in a pan, add fish and cook quickly, turning often, until golden brown. Remove fish and keep warm.
For sauce: Melt butter in another pan, stir in flour and mustard and cook until bubbly, gradually stir in wine and bring to the boil, stirring constantly, until mixture is smooth. Fold in cream and capers and simmer 2–3 minutes. Serve caper sauce over fish.
*(Illustrated on page 31.)*

# Steamed Mussels in Cream Sauce

Serves: 4
Cooking time: 15 minutes

36 mussels
3 tablespoons butter
1 medium onion, chopped
1 stalk celery, finely chopped
½ teaspoon pepper
1 cup (250 ml) white wine
1 cup (250 ml) heavy cream
chopped parsley

Scrub mussels under running water. Melt butter in a flameproof casserole, add onion, celery, pepper, wine and mussels. Cover tightly and simmer 5–6

minutes or until shells are open. Strain off liquid into a pan and boil to reduce liquid to ½ cup. Stir in parsley and cream and heat, do not boil; serve over the mussels.
*(Illustrated on opposite page.)*

# Smoked Haddock with Mustard Sauce

Serves: 4
Cooking time: 50–55 minutes

1½ lbs (750 g) — 4 pieces of smoked haddock
dash of seasoned pepper
juice of 1 lemon
3 cups (750 ml) water
1 large onion, chopped
1 carrot, grated
salt and pepper
1 tablespoon chopped parsley
½ teaspoon thyme
1 bay leaf
1½ tablespoons butter
1½ tablespoons flour
1 teaspoon dry mustard
½ cup (125 ml) wine
½ cup (125 ml) heavy cream
1 egg yolk, beaten
lemon slices
sprigs of parsley

Sprinkle haddock with seasoned pepper and lemon juice and let stand 10 minutes. Combine water, onion, carrot, salt, pepper, chopped parsley, thyme and bay leaf in a pan and boil for 10 minutes. Strain off liquid into another pan, heat and add fish, cover and poach gently for 10–12 minutes. Remove fish carefully and keep hot. Boil liquid to reduce to 1 cup of stock and reserve.
Melt butter in a pan, stir in flour and mustard and cook 1–2 minutes; remove from heat and gradually stir in reserved stock and wine. Return to heat and bring to the boil, stirring constantly; reduce heat and simmer gently until thick and smooth. Fold in cream and egg yolk, heat but do not boil.
Serve smoked haddock with mustard sauce, garnished with lemon slices and parsley sprigs.
*(Illustrated on page 31.)*

STEAMED MUSSELS IN CREAM SAUCE (RECIPE THIS PAGE) ▶

# Creamed Tuna

Serves:   4
Cooking time:   20–25 minutes

15¾ oz (450 g) can of tuna, drained and flaked
4 tablespoons butter
4 scallions, finely chopped
1 small green bell pepper, seeded and finely
   chopped
3 tablespoons flour
salt and pepper
¾ cup (185 ml) white wine
½ cup (125 ml) concentrated fish stock — see
   recipe page 89
¼ cup (65 ml) heavy cream
boiled rice
chopped parsley

Melt 2 tablespoons of butter in a pan, add scallions and bell pepper and sauté until soft, remove vegetables and set aside.

To pan juices add remaining butter and melt, stir in flour, salt and pepper and cook, stirring, for 2–3 minutes, gradually stir in wine and fish stock and bring to the boil, stirring constantly, until thick and smooth. Stir in cooked vegetables and tuna and simmer 2–3 minutes, fold in cream and heat, but do not boil. Serve over boiled rice and sprinkle with parsley.

# Poached Sole in Cream Sauce

Serves:   4
Cooking time:   30–35 minutes
Oven:   180°C   350°F

1½ lbs (750 g) fillets of sole
salt and pepper
4 tablespoons butter
1 clove garlic, crushed
1 large onion, thinly sliced
1 teaspoon black pepper
1 bay leaf
½ cup (125 ml) white wine
¼ cup (65 ml) water
2 tablespoons flour
pinch of salt
dash of cayenne pepper
½ cup (125 ml) heavy cream
chopped parsley

Season fish fillets with salt and pepper and dot with 1 tablespoon of butter; fold fish over and arrange in a greased ovenproof casserole dish. Add garlic, spread fish with onion rings and sprinkle with black pepper; add bay leaf and pour over the wine and water. Cover and cook in a moderate oven for 25 minutes. Strain off liquid and reserve, discard bay leaf and keep fish warm. Melt remaining butter in a pan, add flour, salt and cayenne and cook, stirring, until bubbly, gradually stir in reserved liquid and bring to the boil, stirring constantly, until thick. Fold in cream and heat, but do not boil. Serve cream sauce over fish and sprinkle with parsley.

# Crabmeat in Creôle Sauce

Serves:   4
Cooking time:   30 minutes

15¾ oz (450 g) can of crabmeat, drained and
   flaked
3 tablespoons butter
1 large onion, finely chopped
1 stalk of celery, finely chopped
¼ lb (125 g) mushrooms, chopped
½ teaspoon salt
dash of pepper
1½ tablespoons flour
1 tablespoon paprika
2 teaspoons brown sugar
2 tablespoons malt vinegar
2 tablespoons tomato purée
½ cup (125 ml) cream

Melt butter in a pan, add onion and celery and sauté for 5 minutes, add mushrooms and cook, stirring for 2 minutes. Stir in flour, paprika, salt, pepper and brown sugar and cook 2–3 minutes. Combine vinegar and tomato purée and stir into the pan, cover and simmer gently for 20 minutes. Fold in crabmeat and cream, heat but do not boil. Serve hot.

# Crumbed Trout

Serves: 4
Cooking time: 25–30 minutes
Oven: 200°C 400°F

 2 lbs (1 kg) — 4 small trout
 8 tablespoons butter
 2 tablespoons chopped parsley
 salt and pepper
 1 egg, beaten
 ¼ cup (65 ml) milk
 ½ cup dry breadcrumbs
 ½ cup grated cheese

Melt 2 tablespoons of butter and mix with the parsley and brush it in the cavity of each fish, liberally; season cavity with salt and pepper. Blend egg and milk together and combine breadcrumbs and cheese. Dip each fish in egg mixture, then roll in cheesy breadcrumbs to coat, pressing in well. Grease a baking dish with 1 tablespoon of butter and arrange fish; sprinkle remaining cheesy bread-crumbs on top and dot with remaining butter. Cook in a hot oven for 25 minutes until golden brown.

# Baked Fillets of Fish

Serves: 4
Cooking time: 20 minutes
Oven: 180°C 350°F

 1½ lbs (750 g) — 4 fish fillets
 1 tablespoon oil
 3 tablespoons tomato purée
 ⅓ cup (85 ml) white wine
 2 cloves garlic, slivered
 1 cup soft breadcrumbs
 2 tablespoons chopped parsley
 salt and pepper
 3 tablespoons butter

Line a baking dish with aluminium foil and brush with oil. Arrange fish on the foil. Combine tomato puree and wine and pour this over the fish and top with slivers of garlic. Mix together breadcrumbs and parsley and spread over the fish, sprinkle with salt and pepper and dot with butter. Cook in a moderate oven for 20 minutes.

# Creamed Mushrooms and Trout

Serves: 4
Cooking time: 20–25 minutes

 2 lbs (1 kg) — 4 small trout
 6 tablespoons butter
 ½ teaspoon salt
 ½ lb (250 g) button mushrooms
 2 tablespoons lemon juice
 ½ cup (125 ml) heavy cream
 chopped parsley

Melt butter in a large pan and stir in salt, add fish and cook, turning and basting, for 8–10 minutes; remove fish and keep warm.
To pan juices add mushrooms, and sauté 4–5 minutes; stir in lemon juice and cook 1–2 minutes, stir in cream and heat, stirring, but do not boil. Serve creamed mushrooms over trout and sprinkle with parsley.

# Crumbed Fish Fillets

Serves: 4
Cooking time: 12–15 minutes

 1½ lbs (750 g) fillets of fish
 flour
 salt and pepper
 1 egg, beaten with a little water
 dry breadcrumbs
 oil for frying
 parsley butter — see recipe page 92
 hot tartare sauce — see recipe page 90

Dredge fish fillets with flour seasoned with salt and pepper, dip into egg and toss in dry breadcrumbs. Heat oil in a pan, add fish and cook, turning often, until golden brown all over. Serve fish topped with a pat of parsley butter, with hot tartare sauce on the side.

# Shrimp Stuffed Whiting

Serves: 6
Cooking time: 20–25 minutes
Oven: 190°C 375°F

6 small whole whiting
½ lb (250 g) cooked shrimp, peeled and
    de-veined
½ lb (250 g) button mushrooms, finely sliced
4 tablespoons butter
3 tablespoons parsley
1 teaspoon thyme
2 tablespoons lemon juice
salt and pepper

Clean the fish, remove heads and bones and slit open to lay flat; place fish in a greased, shallow ovenproof casserole dish.

Melt ½ the butter in a pan, add mushrooms and cook 4–5 minutes; remove from heat and add shrimp, parsley, thyme and ½ the lemon juice and stir. Spoon this mixture onto open fish and fold flesh over. Sprinkle remainder of lemon juice over the fish and dot with the remaining butter. Cover and cook in a moderately hot oven for 20–25 minutes.

WHITING IN PARSLEY SAUCE (RECIPE PAGE 38)

SEAFOOD AU GRATIN (RECIPE PAGE 38)

# Seafood au Gratin

Serves:  4–6
Cooking time:   30–35 minutes

 ½ lb (250 g) shrimp, shelled and de-veined
 ½ lb (250 g) scallops, washed and dried
 ½ lb (250 g) fillets of sole
 2 cups (500 ml) court-bouillon — see recipe
   page 88
 ½ cup (125 ml) white wine
 3 tablespoons butter
 1 ½ tablespoons flour
 salt and pepper
 dry breadcrumbs
 grated cheese
 scallop shells, washed and dried

Poach scallops and sole in court-bouillon and wine for 5–6 minutes, remove seafood, flake sole and set aside. Bring liquid to the boil and cook briskly to reduce quantity to 1 cup; strain and reserve.
Melt 1 tablespoon of the butter in a pan, stir in flour, salt and pepper and cook 1–2 minutes; gradually stir in reserved liquid and bring to the boil, stirring constantly, until sauce is thick and smooth.
Place scallop shells on broiler tray. Place portions of shrimp, scallops and sole onto shells (or individual dishes) and spoon white sauce over; sprinkle top with breadcrumbs and cheese and dot with remaining butter. Place tray under the broiler 2″ (5 cm) from high heat and cook 4–5 minutes until tops are golden brown.
(Illustrated on page 37.)

# Oysters Mornay

Serves:  4
Cooking time:   15 minutes

 24 oysters on the shell for 4 persons
 3 tablespoons butter
 3 tablespoons flour
 1 ¼ cups (300 ml) hot milk
 salt and pepper
 ½ cup grated cheese

Arrange oyster shells on a broiler tray. Melt butter in a pan, stir in flour and cook until bubbly, remove from heat and stir in the hot milk; return to heat and cook, stirring constantly, until boiling, reduce heat and simmer 2 minutes. Add salt, pepper and fold in ⅔ of the cheese, cook over gentle heat until cheese has melted. Spoon sauce over oysters, top with remaining cheese and cook under broiler until golden brown.

# Whiting in Parsley Sauce

Serves:  4
Cooking time:   20–25 minutes

 1 ½ lbs (750 g) fillets of whiting
 flour
 salt and pepper
 1 egg beaten with a little water
 3 tablespoons dry breadcrumbs
 1 tablespoon chopped parsley
 2 tablespoons oil
 4 tablespoons butter
 ½ cup (125 ml) milk
 ½ cup (125 ml) heavy cream
 1 tablespoon chives, chopped finely

Dredge fish fillets in flour seasoned with salt and pepper, dip in egg and roll in mixture of breadcrumbs and parsley. Heat oil and 2 tablespoons butter in a pan, add fish and brown on all sides; remove fish and keep warm.
In another pan melt remaining 2 tablespoons of butter, stir in 1 tablespoon of leftover seasoned flour and cook 1–2 minutes; gradually stir in milk and bring to the boil, stirring constantly. Remove from heat and fold in cream; return to heat and warm.
Serve fish with white sauce spooned over and sprinkled with chives.
(Illustrated on page 37.)

# Pickled Fish

Serves: 6
Cooking time: 15 minutes

2 lbs (1 kg) fillets of fish
3 tablespoons butter
4 scallions, finely chopped
1 clove garlic, crushed
2 oranges
¼ cup (65 ml) salad oil
3 tablespoons tarragon vinegar
salt and pepper
1 small green bell pepper, seeded and finely
   sliced
2 bay leaves
1 tablespoon chopped parsley.

Melt butter in a pan, add fish, cover and simmer gently for 8–10 minutes. Remove fish and arrange in a glass dish. To pan juices add scallions and garlic and sauté until scallions are soft, then set aside. Remove rind from oranges in strips and squeeze the juice.
In a blender combine orange juice, salad oil, vinegar, salt and pepper and blend 2–3 minutes, pour into the pan with scallions and garlic, stir and heat, add orange rind, bay leaves and parsley. Stir and spoon over the fish. Cover tightly and refrigerate for 12 hours, or over night, basting fish with the liquid occasionally. Discard bay leaves and serve fish cold with a salad.

# Cream of Oyster Soup

Serves: 4
Cooking time: 15–20 minutes

8 oz (225 g) can of whole oysters, drained
4 tablespoons butter
4 tablespoons flour
2 cups (500 ml) concentrated fish stock — see
   recipe page 89
1 cup (250 ml) milk
salt and pepper
¾ cup (185 ml) heavy cream
2 teaspoons chopped chives
paprika
chopped parsley

Melt butter in a pan, stir in flour, salt and pepper and cook, stirring, until bubbly. Remove pan from heat and gradually stir in fish stock and milk. Return to heat and bring to the boil, stirring constantly, until thick and smooth. Fold in oysters, cream and chives and heat, but do not boil. Serve soup sprinkled with paprika and parsley.

# Fish Fingers with Hot Tartare Sauce

Serves: 4
Cooking time: 10 minutes

frozen fish fingers for 4 persons
1½ tablespoons butter
1 small onion, minced
1½ tablespoons cornstarch
1 cup (250 ml) milk
2 tablespoons mayonnaise
2 teaspoons capers, minced
1 tablespoon chopped parsley
salt and pepper

Heat fish fingers as directed on package. Melt butter in a pan, add onion and sauté until soft, stir in cornstarch until smooth. Gradually stir in milk and bring to the boil, stirring constantly, and simmer until thick and smooth. Fold in mayonnaise, capers, parsley, salt and pepper and heat.
Serve hot tartare sauce over fish fingers.

# Oysters Kilpatrick

Serves: 4
Cooking time: 6–8 minutes

24 oysters on the shell for 4 persons
salt and pepper
4 slices of lean bacon, finely chopped
4 tablespoons Worcestershire sauce
chopped parsley

Arrange oyster shells on a broiler tray, sprinkle each oyster with salt and pepper, ½ teaspoon of chopped bacon and ½ teaspoon of Worcestershire sauce. Place tray under hot broiler and cook until bacon is crisp.
Serve oysters sprinkled with parsley.

# Seafood in White Sauce

Serves: 4–6
Cooking time: 25–30 minutes

*1½ lbs (750 g) cooked lobster*
*½ lb (250 g) cooked shrimp*
*1 cup (250 ml) milk*
*1 small onion stuck with 4 cloves*
*1 bay leaf*
*4 tablespoons butter*
*3 tablespoons flour*
*1 medium onion, sliced*
*2 scallions, finely chopped*
*½ teaspoon prepared mustard*
*salt and pepper*
*½ cup (125 ml) white wine*
*½ cup (125 ml) cream*

Cut lobster in half, remove flesh and cut into pieces and place in a flameproof casserole. Reserve 6 shrimp for garnish; shell and de-vein the remainder and add to the lobster. In a pan combine milk with onion, stuck with cloves, and bay leaf; bring to the boil and simmer 2–3 minutes, strain and reserve the liquid.

Melt 2 tablespoons of butter in a pan, stir in flour, remove pan from heat and gradually stir in reserved milk liquid. Return pan to heat and cook, stirring constantly, until mixture reaches the boil and thickens into a white sauce, then set aside.

Melt remaining 1 tablespoon of butter in a pan, add scallions and onion and sauté until soft, stir in mustard, salt and pepper and gradually stir in wine and bring to the boil; fold in white sauce and cream, heat and pour over seafood. Cover and cook gently for 5–6 minutes.

Serve garnished with 6 shrimp.

FISH WITH CIDER SAUCE (RECIPE PAGE 42) ▶

# Oysters Bordelaise

Serves: 4
Cooking time: 15 minutes
Oven: 200°C 400°F

*24 oysters on the shell for 4 persons*
*3 tablespoons butter*
*2 scallions, finely chopped*
*salt and pepper*
*1 teaspoon paprika*
*¼ cup (65 ml) red wine*
*dry breadcrumbs*

Arrange oyster shells on an oven tray. Melt 1 tablespoon of butter in a pan, add scallions and sauté until soft, add salt, pepper, paprika and wine and cook, stirring, until boiling. Spoon sauce over oysters, sprinkle with breadcrumbs and dot with remaining butter. Cook in a hot oven for 10 minutes.

# Fish Patties

Serves: 4
Cooking time: 20–25 minutes

*1 lb (500 g) fillets of fish*
*¾ cup (185 ml) concentrated fish stock — see*
  *recipe page 89*
*1½ tablespoons butter or margarine*
*½ teaspoon dry mustard*
*1½ tablespoons flour*
*salt and pepper*
*¼ cup (65 ml) milk*
*1 cup cooked mashed potatoes*
*extra flour*
*1 egg, beaten with a little water*
*dry breadcrumbs*
*oil for frying*
*chopped parsley*

Arrange fish in a pan, add stock, cover and simmer gently for 8–10 minutes, strain off liquid and reserve; flake fish and set aside.
Melt butter or margarine in a pan, stir in flour and cook 1–2 minutes, gradually stir in reserved liquid, then the milk, and bring to the boil, stirring constantly, and simmer until thick and smooth. Fold in fish and mashed potatoes and set aside to cool. Divide mixture into 8 equal portions and shape into patties, dust with flour, dip in egg and toss in breadcrumbs to coat. Cook in hot oil, turning often, until golden brown, drain on paper towels and serve sprinkled with parsley.

# Fish with Cider Sauce

Serves: 4
Cooking time: 20–25 minutes

*1½ lbs (750 g) fish fillets*
*flour*
*salt and pepper*
*oil for frying*

**Sauce:**
*1½ tablespoons butter*
*1½ tablespoons flour*
*salt*
*seasoned pepper*
*1 cup (250 ml) cider or sauterne*

*shredded carrots, steamed*
*new potatoes, boiled*
*cabbage and leek, sliced and boiled*

Coat fish fillets with flour seasoned with salt and pepper. Heat oil in a pan, add fish and cook quickly to brown all over.
For sauce: Melt butter in a pan, stir in flour, salt and seasoned pepper and cook until lightly browned. Gradually stir in cider and, stirring constantly, bring to the boil and cook until mixture is smooth.
Serve fillets with sauce and vegetables.
*(Illustrated page 41.)*

# Fish Soup with Saffron

Serves:  4
Cooking time:  50–55 minutes

> 1½ lbs (750 g) fish steaks
> 4 cups (1 liter) wine court-bouillon — see recipe
>   page 88
> 4 tablespoons butter
> 1 medium onion, finely chopped
> 1 clove garlic, crushed
> ½ lb (250 g) tomatoes, peeled and chopped
> 1 tablespoon chopped parsley
> 1 tablespoon chopped chives
> 1 bouquet garni
> salt and pepper
> dash of nutmeg
> 1 teaspoon thyme
> 1 teaspoon saffron
> 2 cups (500 ml) milk
> 1 cup (250 ml) heavy cream
> toast

Heat court-bouillon to boiling in a deep pan, add the fish, reduce heat, cover and simmer for 10 minutes. In a separate pan melt the butter, add onion and garlic and sauté until lightly browned, stir in tomatoes and cook, stirring, for 5–6 minutes. Add parsley, chives, salt, pepper, nutmeg and thyme and cook, stirring, for 2–3 minutes. Pour mixture over the fish, add bouquet garni, cover and simmer for 25 minutes. Remove fish and cut into small pieces and keep warm.

Strain off liquid into a flameproof casserole dish, add saffron and milk and bring to the boil and simmer for 5–6 minutes. Fold in fish pieces and cream and heat, but do not boil. Serve pieces of fish in each bowl and ladle soup over.

# Oysters Czarina

Serves:  4

> 24 oysters on the shell for 4 persons
> 4 teaspoons caviar
> 2 tablespoons lemon juice
> pepper
> chopped parsley
> lemon wedges

On each oyster place a little caviar, sprinkle with lemon juice, pepper and parsley. Serve with lemon wedges.

# Fish Mornay

Serves:  4
Cooking time:  35–40 minutes
Oven:  180°C  350°F

> 1½ lbs (750 g) fillets of halibut, cut in small
> pieces
> juice of 1 lemon
> salt and seasoned pepper
> 3 tablespoons butter
> 1 medium onion, chopped
> 1½ tablespoons flour
> 1 cup (250 ml) milk
> 3 tablespoons grated cheese

Place fish pieces in a greased ovenproof casserole dish, sprinkle with lemon juice, salt and pepper and let stand for 1 hour. Drain off liquid and reserve. Melt 1 tablespoon of butter in a pan, add onion and sauté until transparent, stir in flour and cook 1–2 minutes, gradually stir in reserved liquid and milk and bring to the boil, stirring constantly, and simmer until sauce has thickened. Fold in half the cheese and pour mixture over the fish. Top with remaining cheese and dot with remaining butter. Cook in a moderate oven for 25 minutes until top is golden brown.

# Fish Pie

Serves: 6–8
Cooking time: 45–50 minutes
Oven: 190°C 375°F

*1½ lbs (750 g) fish fillets*
*½ cup (125 ml) white wine*
*salt and seasoned pepper*
*1 bay leaf*
*1½ tablespoons butter*
*1½ tablespoons flour*
*¾ cup (185 ml) milk*
*2 eggs, beaten*
*3 tablespoons grated cheese*

**Pastry:**
*1 cup flour*
*1 teaspoon salt*
*dash of pepper*
*4 tablespoons butter*
*1 egg yolk*
*1 tablespoon lemon juice*
*1 tablespoon water*
*extra flour*

To make pastry: Sift 1 cup flour, salt and pepper in a bowl, add butter and rub in well with fingers until mixture is like fine breadcrumbs. Combine egg, lemon juice and water, add to the flour and mix into a light dough and allow to stand for 15–20 minutes. Roll out pastry on a floured board and line a greased 23 cm (8″) pie dish, prick base and cook in a moderately hot oven for 8–10 minutes.

Meanwhile, combine wine, salt, seasoned pepper and bay leaf in a pan, add fish and poach for 8–10 minutes. Remove fish, flake and set aside; strain liquid and boil to reduce to ¼ cup and reserve.

Melt butter in a pan, stir in flour and cook 1–2 minutes. Gradually stir in milk and bring to the boil, stirring constantly, and cook until thick. Stir in reserved liquid, remove from heat and fold in eggs and fish. Turn into the pastry and sprinkle with cheese. Cook in a moderately hot oven for 25–30 minutes.

Serve hot or cold.

SEASONED LOBSTER IN PASTRY (RECIPE PAGE 46)

STUFFED HERRINGS (RECIPE PAGE 46)

# Stuffed Herring

Serves: 4
Cooking time: 30–40 minutes

1½ lbs (750 g) herring, without heads
8 anchovies, chopped
1 small onion, chopped
½ teaspoon salt
4 tablespoons tomato paste
4 tablespoons flour
¼ cup (65 ml) milk
5 tablespoons dry breadcrumbs
4 tablespoons butter
¼ cup (65 ml) white wine
¼ cup (65 ml) heavy cream
chopped parsley

Rinse fish with water and pat dry. Combine anchovies, onion, salt and 1 tablespoon tomato paste and press some into the cavity of each fish. Dust fish with flour, dip in milk and roll in breadcrumbs. Heat 2 tablespoons butter in a flameproof casserole, add fish and brown on all sides. Remove fish and set aside. To pan juices add remaining 1 tablespoon butter and heat, stir in leftover flour and cook 1–2 minutes. Stir in remaining tomato paste and wine. Cook, stirring constantly, until smooth and thick. Fold in cream and return fish. Cover and simmer gently for 15 minutes. Serve sprinkled with parsley.
(Illustrated on page 45.)

# Shrimp Curry and Rice

Serves: 4
Cooking time: 25–30 minutes

1 lb (500 g) shelled and de-veined shrimp
1 tablespoon curry powder
1 teaspoon salt
2 tablespoons vinegar
2 tablespoons oil
1 large onion, finely chopped
½ lb (250 g) tomatoes, peeled and chopped
½ cup (125 ml) sour cream
boiled rice
chopped parsley

In a bowl combine curry powder salt and vinegar. Add shrimp, stir to coat and let stand to marinate for 1½ hours, stirring occasionally.
Heat oil in a pan, add onion and sauté until golden brown, add tomatoes and cook for 5–6 minutes. Add shrimp and marinade and cook, stirring constantly, for 2–3 minutes. Reduce heat, cover and simmer gently for 15 minutes. Fold in sour cream and heat, but do not boil.
Serve shrimp curry over boiled rice and sprinkle with parsley.

# Seasoned Lobster in Pastry

Serves: 4
Cooking time: 20 minutes
Oven: 200° 400°F

1½ lbs (750 g) cooked lobster
½ cup soft breadcrumbs
1 small onion, finely chopped
2 teaspoons chopped parsley
salt and pepper
1 teaspoon mixed herbs
¼ cup (65 ml) white wine
2 tablespoons mayonnaise
12 oz (375 g) packet frozen puff pastry, thawed
1 egg yolk, beaten
lettuce leaves
hot tartare sauce — see recipe page 90

Split lobster in half, remove flesh from the body and claws and cut into bite size pieces. Combine breadcrumbs, onion, parsley, salt, pepper, mixed herbs and wine in a bowl and mix to make seasoning.
Divide pastry into 4 equal portions and roll out. On each portion place ¼ of the seasoning and ¼ of the lobster and spoon over ¼ of the mayonnaise. Wrap the pastry around the filling and tuck in the ends and seal; place on a greased baking tray and brush with egg. Cook in a hot oven for 20 minutes until golden brown.
Serve hot or cold with lettuce leaves and hot or cold tartare sauce.
(Illustrated on page 45.)

# Salmon au Gratin

Serves: 4
Cooking time: 35 minutes
Oven: 180°C 350°F

15¾ oz (450 g) can pink salmon
4 tablespoons butter
1 medium onion, finely chopped
3 tablespoons flour
½ cup (125 ml) white wine
½ cup (125 ml) milk
6 tablespoons grated cheese
juice of 1 lemon
salt and pepper
½ cup (125 ml) heavy cream
dry breadcrumbs

Drain and flake the salmon. Melt 2 tablespoons butter in a pan, add onion and sauté until soft, stir in flour and cook until bubbly, gradually stir in wine, then the milk, bring to the boil, stirring constantly, until thick and smooth. Stir in ½ the cheese, the lemon juice, salt, pepper and salmon, heat, then fold in cream.

Turn into a greased ovenproof casserole dish, top with breadcrumbs and remaining cheese and dot with remaining butter. Cook in a moderate oven for 25–30 minutes until golden brown.

# Shrimp Cocktail

Serves: 4
No cooking

1½ lbs (750 g) shrimp, shelled and de-veined
3 tablespoons mayonnaise
2 tablespoons tomato catsup
1 teaspoon Worcestershire sauce
dash of tabasco sauce
salt and pepper
¼ cup (65 ml) heavy cream
2 lettuce leaves, shredded
½ stalk celery, finely chopped
chopped parsley
lemon wedges

Combine mayonnaise, tomato, Worcestershire and Tabasco sauces with salt, pepper and cream and mix to a smooth sauce.

In serving bowls place lettuce and celery and arrange shrimp on top. Spoon sauce over shrimp and sprinkle with parsley. Serve with lemon wedges.

# Flounder in White Sauce

Serves: 4
Cooking time: 35–40 minutes
Oven: 180°C 350°F

1½ lbs (750 g) fillets of flounder
1 tablespoon lemon juice
salt and seasoned pepper
1 large onion, sliced in rings
1 bay leaf
½ cup (125 ml) water
½ cup (125 ml) white wine
1½ tablespoons butter
1 medium onion, finely chopped
1½ tablespoons flour
1 cup (250 ml) milk
1 tablespoon chopped parsley

Roll fish fillets and secure with toothpicks. Arrange in an ovenproof casserole dish, sprinkle with lemon juice, salt and pepper; add onion rings, bay leaf, water and wine. Cover and cook in a moderate oven for 25 minutes. Drain off the liquid into a pan and boil briskly to reduce to ¼ cup (65 ml) and reserve. Discard bay leaf from casserole and keep fish hot.

Meanwhile, melt butter in a pan, add chopped onion and sauté until transparent, stir in flour and cook 1–2 minutes, gradually stir in milk and bring to the boil, stirring constantly, until thick and smooth. Stir in reserved liquid and simmer for 4–5 minutes.

Serve white sauce over fish and sprinkle with parsley.

# Baked Mullet with Potato Puffs

Serves: 4–6
Cooking time: 40 minutes
Oven: 180°C 350°F

1 large mullet
1 lemon
salt and pepper
½ cup (125 ml) rosé
½ cup (125 ml) dry white wine
½ cup (125 ml) water
1 egg, beaten
¼ cup (65 ml) heavy cream
sprig of parsley
lemon slices

**Potato Puffs:**
3 cups cooked mashed potatoes, chilled
½ cup flour, sifted
pinch salt
⅓ cup (85 ml) lukewarm water
1 egg, separated
2 tablespoons olive or salad oil
oil for frying

Rub cavity of the mullet with a wedge of the lemon and season with salt and pepper. Place fish in a greased, shallow, ovenproof casserole dish and squeeze over the juice from the remainder of the lemon; let stand 15 minutes. Pour rosé, wine and water over the fish, cover tightly and cook in a moderate oven 35–40 minutes. Remove fish and keep hot, reserve liquid. Combine egg and cream and beat, gradually stir into the reserved liquid and heat, but do not boil.

Meanwhile to make potato puffs: mix flour, salt and water together and beat until smooth; beat in egg yolk and oil. Beat egg whites until stiff then fold into the batter. Let batter stand 15 minutes. Heat oil in a deep pan. Scoop spoonfuls of mashed potato and drop into the batter. Use a slotted spoon to lift and drain potato. Slowly lower potato balls into hot oil, one at a time; they rise to the surface when cooked and golden brown.

Serve baked mullet with potato puffs, garnished with lemon slices and sprig of parsley.

COD ON ZUCCHINI & TOMATOES (RECIPE PAGE 50) ▶

# Salmon Mousse

Serves: 4
No cooking

    2 × 15½ oz (440 g) cans salmon, drained and
      flaked
    1 enveloped of gelatin
    ¼ cup (65 ml) white wine
    ¼ cup (65 ml) boiling water
    ¼ cup mayonnaise
    1 tablespoon lemon juice
    1 tablespoon minced onion
    dash of Tabasco sauce
    dash of paprika
    salt and pepper
    ½ cup (125 ml) heavy cream
    1 dill pickle, finely chopped

Pour wine into a bowl, sprinkle gelatin on top and let stand 5 minutes to soften. Add the boiling water and stir until gelatin is dissolved, then cool. Stir in mayonnaise, lemon juice, onion, Tabasco sauce, paprika, salt and pepper and mix thoroughly; chill for 15–20 minutes.
Blend salmon with half the cream to a purée.
Beat the remaining cream until stiff and fold into the salmon puree, add dill pickle and stir. Fold salmon purée into gelatin mixture and stir. Spoon salmon mousse into a greased mold and refrigerate for at least 2 hours. Turn mousse out onto a platter and serve with a salad.

# Cod on Zucchini and Tomatoes

Serves: 4
Cooking time: 25–30 minutes

    1½ lbs (750 g) — 4 cod steaks
    3 tablespoons oil
    1 medium onion, chopped
    1 clove garlic, crushed
    1 lb (500 g) zucchini, sliced
    1 lb (500 g) tomatoes, chopped
    1 green bell pepper, seeded and thinly sliced
    salt and pepper
    juice of 1 lemon
    ½ cup (125 ml) white wine

Heat oil in a pan, add onions, garlic, zucchini, tomatoes, green pepper, salt and pepper and cook, stirring gently, for 5–6 minutes. Add fish, sprinkle with lemon juice and wine. Cover tightly and simmer gently for 15–20 minutes.
(Illustrated on page 49.)

# Garlic Prawns

Serves: 4
Cooking time: 15–20 minutes

    1½ lbs (750 g) or shrimp, shelled and de-veined
    4 tablespoons butter
    1 medium onion, minced
    3 cloves garlic, crushed
    salt and pepper
    chopped parsley
    ½ cup (125 ml) vermouth

Melt butter in a pan, add onion and garlic and sauté until golden, stir in salt, pepper and parsley and add prawns. Cook, stirring, until prawns are pink, 6–7 minutes, stir in vermouth and simmer 3–4 minutes.
Serve bubbly hot on boiled rice.

# Savoury Shrimp on Rice

Serves: 4
Cooking time: 10–12 minutes

    2 lbs (1 kg) shrimp, shelled and de-veined
    ½ teaspoon prepared hot mustard
    dash of cayenne pepper
    ½ cup tomato sauce
    2 teaspoons Worcestershire sauce
    1 tablespoon lemon juice
    ½ cup (125 ml) water
    1½ tablespoons cornstarch
    boiled rice
    chopped parsley

Combine mustard, cayenne, tomato and Worcestershire sauces, lemon juice and water in a pan and bring to the boil, stirring. Mix cornstarch with a little water and stir into sauce to thicken and simmer 1–2 minutes, and shrimp, cover and simmer very gently for 4–5 minutes. Serve over hot rice and sprinkle with parsley.

# Salmon Loaf

Serves:  4
Cooking time:  30 minutes
Oven:  180°C  350°F

15¾ oz (450 g) can of pink salmon, drained and
   flaked
1 large onion, finely chopped
2 eggs
1½ cups soft breadcrumbs
15¾ oz (450 g) can cream of celery soup
salt and pepper
1 tablespoon chopped parsley
2 tablespoon white wine
1½ tablespoons butter

Combine salmon in a bowl with onion, eggs and
breadcrumbs. Stir in celery soup, salt, pepper,
parsley and wine.
Grease a loaf tin and add mixture, pressing lightly
to firm; dot with butter and cook in a moderate oven
for 30 minutes. Serve hot or cold.

# Savoury Ocean Perch

Serves:  4
Cooking time:  20–25 minutes

1½ lbs (750 g) fillets of ocean perch
flour
salt and pepper
oil for frying
3 tablespoons butter or margarine
1 large onion, chopped
1 clove garlic, crushed
1 large tomato, peeled and chopped
1 tablespoon chopped parsley

Dredge fish fillets in flour seasoned with salt and
pepper. Heat oil in a pan, add fish and cook until
golden brown, remove fish and keep hot.
Melt butter in a pan, add onion and sauté until
transparent: add garlic, tomato, salt, pepper and
parsley and cook, stirring, for 5 minutes. Cover and
simmer gently for 10 minutes, then stir briskly.
Serve over fillets of ocean perch.

# Potato Topped Tuna Pie

Serves:  4
Cooking time:  35–40 minutes
Oven:  180°C  350°F

15¾ oz (450 g) can tuna, drained and flaked
4 tablespoons butter
1 medium onion, finely chopped
12 oz (375 g) can cream of celery soup
½ cup (125 ml) white wine
¼ cup (65 ml) lemon juice
salt and pepper
2 cups cooked and mashed potatoes

Melt half the butter in a pan, add onion and sauté
until soft. In a bowl combine tuna with celery soup,
wine, lemon juice, salt and pepper, add cooked
onion and pan juices and mix thoroughly. Turn into
a greased ovenproof casserole dish and cover with
mashed potatoes. Dot with remaining butter and
cook in a moderate oven for 30 minutes until
golden brown.

# Fried Mullet with Lemon Caper Sauce

Serves:  4
Cooking time:  15–20 minutes

1½ lbs (750 g) fillets of mullet
4 tablespoons lemon juice
flour
salt and pepper
4 tablespoons butter
2 tablespoons capers, chopped
1 tablespoon chopped parsley

Brush fish fillets with half the lemon juice and dust
with flour seasoned with salt and pepper. Melt 2
tablespoons of butter in a pan, add fish and cook
until golden brown all over, remove fish and keep
warm.
To pan juices add remaining 1 tablespoon of butter
and heat, add capers, parsley and remainder of
lemon juice, cook over gentle heat for 3 minutes.
Serve lemon caper sauce over fish fillets.

# Crab on Pastry with Shrimp

Serves: 4
Cooking time: 20–25 minutes
Oven: 200°C 400°F

15¾ oz (450 g) can of crab meat, drained and
  flaked
flaky pastry sheets, prepared
¾ cup (185 g) butter, melted
1½ tablespoons extra butter
1 small onion, minced
salt and pepper
2 tablespoons brandy
½ lb (250 g) cooked shrimp

For the pastry use 4 sheets of prepared pastry. Brush each pastry sheet with melted butter and stack one on top of the other; fold pastry sheets in half, butter, then fold again in half, which will make a strip approximately 4½″ × 11″ (11 cm × 28 cm). Cut the strip into 4 equal parts and brush tops with butter. Place pastry squares on a greased oven tray. Cook in a hot oven for 10 minutes; turn pastry over carefully, brush tops with butter and cook a further 10 minutes until golden brown. Remove pastry and allow to cool.

Meanwhile melt the extra 20 g butter in a pan, add onion and sauté until transparent, stir in brandy, salt and pepper and simmer 2–3 minutes. Fold in crab meat and heat, stirring. Turn mixture into a bowl and chill.

Serve pastry squares topped with crab mixture and garnished with shrimp.

52

FISH FILLETS WITH MUSTARD SAUCE (RECIPE PAGE 54)

FISH AND POTATO PIE (RECIPE PAGE 54)

# Fish and Potato Pie

Serves:   4
Cooking time:   25–30 minutes
Oven:   200°C   400°F

1 lb (500 g) fish fillets, steamed and diced
3 tablespoons butter
2 medium onions, chopped finely
1 clove garlic, crushed
4 tablespoons chopped parsley
salt and pepper
½ cup (125 ml) white wine or water
3 cups cooked, mashed potatoes
¼ cup (65 ml) milk
grated cheese

Melt butter in a pan, add onion and garlic and sauté until transparent; remove from heat and add parsley, salt, pepper, fish and wine or water and mix all together. Turn mixture into a greased ovenproof casserole dish and top with mashed potatoes to completely cover. Brush top with milk and sprinkle liberally with grated cheese. Cook in a hot oven for 20 minutes or until top is golden brown.
(Illustrated on page 53.)

# Fish Fillets with Mustard Sauce

Serves:   4
Cooking time:   20 minutes

1½ lbs (750 g) fillets of flounder or halibut
2 cups (500 ml) court-bouillon — see recipe
    page 88
3 tablespoons butter
3 tablespoons grated cheese
1 mandarin, in segments
pastry crescent garnish
lemon wedges

**Sauce:**
2 teaspoons prepared mustard
8 tablespoons butter, melted

Place fish in a pan and pour over the court-bouillon, bring to the boil and simmer gently for 5 minutes. Remove fish carefully, drain and place on aluminium foil with mandarin segments; brush fish with butter and sprinkle with cheese; place under a broiler to brown for about 6 minutes.
Meanwhile, for the sauce: Mix mustard and melted butter together in a pan until smooth, and heat.
Serve fish with mustard sauce poured over, garnished with pastry crescents and lemon wedges.
(Illustrated on page 53.)

# Curried Fish Fillets

Serves:   4
Cooking time:   40 minutes
Oven:   180°C   350°F

1 lb (500 g) filleted fish, diced
2 tablespoons shredded coconut
1½ cups (375 ml) concentrated fish stock — see
    recipe page 89
4 tablespoons butter
2 medium onions, chopped
1 cooking apple, peeled, cored and chopped
3 tablespoons flour
1 tablespoon curry powder
3 tablespoons fruit chutney
salt
dash of cayenne pepper
1 tablespoon lemon juice
boiled rice
chopped parsley

Combine coconut and fish stock in a bowl and let stand for 20 minutes.
Melt butter in a pan, add onions and apple and sauté 3–4 minutes; stir in flour, curry, fruit chutney, salt and cayenne and cook, stirring 3–4 minutes. Stir in coconut stock and lemon juice and bring to the boil, stirring constantly.
Place fish in an ovenproof casserole dish and pour over the curry sauce, cover and cook in a moderate oven for 30 minutes. Serve fish over boiled rice and sprinkle with parsley.

# Scallops in Spiced Wine

Serves: 4
Cooking time: 15 minutes

1½ lbs (750 g) scallops
1 teaspoon French mustard
½ teaspoon thyme
dash of sage
pinch of salt
½ cup (125 ml) white wine
3 tablespoons butter
4 scallions, finely chopped
clove garlic, crushed
1 tablespoon chopped parsley

Combine mustard, thyme, sage, salt and wine and mix well. Melt butter in a pan, add scallions and garlic and sauté until soft, stir in spiced wine and bring to the boil. Reduce heat, add scallops and parsley and simmer, stirring occasionally, for 8–10 minutes. Serve at once.

# Fried Scallops

Serves: 4
Cooking time: 15 minutes

1½ lbs (750 g) scallops
flour
salt and pepper
1 egg, beaten with a little water
dry breadcrumbs
oil for cooking
chopped parsley
hot tartare sauce — see recipe page 90
lemon wedges

Dredge scallops in flour seasoned with salt and pepper, dip into egg and toss in breadcrumbs to coat. Chill for at least ½ hour.
Heat oil in a pan, add scallops and cook, turning often until golden brown all over, drain on paper towels. Serve sprinkled with parsley, garnished with lemon wedges and hot tartare sauce on the side.

# Curried Shrimp

Serves: 4
Cooking time: 25–30 minutes

1 lb (500 g) shelled and de-veined shrimp
3 tablespoons butter
1 large onion, finely chopped
1 stalk of celery, finely chopped
1 tablespoon ginger
1 tablespoon curry powder
1 teaspoon dry mustard
½ teaspoon turmeric
1 teaspoon salt
dash of seasoned pepper
1 tablespoon cornstarch
1 cup (250 ml) chicken cube stock
½ cup (125 ml) white wine
2 tablespoons lemon juice

Melt butter in a pan, add onion and sauté until golden, add celery and cook, stirring, 2–3 minutes. Stir in ginger, curry, mustard, turmeric, salt, pepper and cornstarch, then gradually stir in stock and wine. Bring to the boil, stirring constantly. Lower heat and simmer gently, stirring occasionally, for 20 minutes. Add shrimp and lemon juice and simmer for 5 minutes. Serve on boiled rice sprinkled with parsley.

# Scallops in Tarragon Butter Sauce

Serves: 4
Cooking time: 15 minutes

1½ (750 g) scallops
6 tablespoons butter
2 teaspoons tarragon
4 scallions, finely chopped
3 tablespoons white wine
salt and pepper
chopped parsley

Melt butter in a pan, add tarragon and scallions and sauté until tender, stir in wine and cook 1–2 minutes. Add scallops, and stir, cover and simmer gently for 5 minutes, uncover and simmer 2–3 minutes longer. Serve sprinkled with parsley.

# Fish Fritters

Serves: 4
Cooking time: 15–20 minutes

4 small whole fish
6 tablespoons sifted flour
4 tablespoons milk
1 egg
salt and pepper
oil for frying
3 tablespoons butter
1 clove garlic, crushed
½ teaspoon seasoned pepper
4 tablespoons brandy
1 lemon, sliced in rings
chopped parsley

Combine flour, milk, egg, salt and pepper and beat until smooth; dip the fish in to coat all over. Heat oil in a pan, when hot add fish and cook quickly, turning, until golden brown on all sides. Remove fish and keep warm.

Melt butter in another pan, add garlic and seasoned pepper and cook, stirring, 1–2 minutes; gradually stir in brandy and, still stirring, heat. Pour brandy sauce over fish and serve with lemon rings dredged in parsley.

56

FISH STEAKS WITH PIQUANT SAUCE (RECIPE PAGE 58) ▶

# Fish Steaks with Piquant Sauce

Serves: 4
Cooking time: 35 minutes

 4 fish steaks 1" (2½ cm) thick
 ½ lb (250 g) lean bacon strips
 1½ tablespoons butter
 1 clove garlic, crushed
 salt and seasoned pepper
 1½ tablespoons flour
 ¼ lb (125 g) mushrooms, chopped
 ½ teaspoon tarragon
 1 tablespoon chopped parsley
 2 tablespoons lemon juice
 ½ cup (125 ml) white wine

Cook bacon in a pan until crisp, remove and keep warm. Add butter to the pan juices and heat, add garlic, salt, pepper and flour and, stirring, cook 1–2 minutes. Stir in mushrooms, tarragon, parsley, lemon juice and wine and bring to the boil. Add fish steaks and spoon sauce over; cover tightly and simmer gently for 15–18 minutes.
Serve fish steaks and bacon and spoon sauce over.
*(Illustrated on page 57.)*

# Scallops in Cheese Sauce

Serves: 4
Cooking time: 25–30 minutes

 1½ lbs (750 g) scallops
 4 tablespoons butter
 2 tablespoons chopped parsley
 salt and pepper
 1½ tablespoons flour
 ¾ cup (185 ml) white wine
 ¼ cup (65 ml) water
 3 tablespoons grated cheese
 1 tablespoon chopped chives
 ½ cup (125 ml) cream

Melt 2 tablespoons butter in a pan, add scallops and ½ the parsley and sauté gently for 8–10 minutes, season with salt and pepper; remove scallops and keep warm.
To pan juices add remaining butter and melt, stir in flour and cook, stirring, for 1–2 minutes, gradually stir in wine and water and bring to the boil, stirring constantly and cook until thick and smooth. Stir in cheese, chives and scallops and simmer 4–5 minutes. Fold in cream and heat, but do not boil. Serve sprinkled with remaining parsley.

# Snapper in White Wine

Serves: 4
Cooking time: 40 minutes
Oven: 180°C 350°F

 2 lbs (1 kg) — 4 small snapper
 6 tablespoons salad oil
 salt and pepper
 1 medium onion, chopped
 1 clove garlic, crushed
 1 stalk of celery, chopped
 4 strips of bacon, chopped
 2 large tomatoes, peeled and chopped
 1 small bell pepper, seeded and chopped
 1 tablespoon chopped parsley
 1 teaspoon oregano
 ¾ cup (185 ml) white wine

Brush each fish with oil, sprinkle with salt and pepper and arrange in a greased ovenproof casserole dish.
Heat oil in a pan, add onion and garlic and sauté 1–2 minutes, add celery, bacon, tomatoes and bell pepper, cover and cook gently for 5 minutes, stir in parsley, oregano and wine, heat and spoon over the fish. Cover and cook in a moderate oven for 30 minutes.

# Snapper in Beer

Serves: 4–6
Cooking time: 35 minutes
Oven: 180°C 350°F

> 2 lbs (1 kg) snapper fillets
> 3 tablespoons butter
> 1 large onion, finely chopped
> 1 tablespoon grated lemon rind
> juice of 1 lemon
> salt and pepper
> 1 extra medium onion, sliced in rings
> ¾ cup (185 ml) flat beer

Line a baking dish with aluminium foil and brush with 1 tablespoon melted butter, spread chopped onion and lemon rind on base and arrange fish on top, sprinkle fish with lemon juice, salt and pepper and dot with remaining butter. Place onion rings on top and pour the beer over. Cover tightly with foil and cook in a moderate oven for 35 minutes.

# Snapper Casserole

Serves: 4
Cooking time: 30 minutes
Oven: 180°C 350°F

> 1½ lbs (750 g) — 4 fillets of snapper
> salt and seasoned pepper
> grated rind and juice of 1 lemon
> 3 scallions, finely chopped
> 2 large tomatoes, peeled and sliced
> 3 tablespoons dry breadcrumbs
> 3 tablespoons grated cheese
> 3 tablespoons butter

Arrange fish fillets in a greased ovenproof casserole dish and sprinkle with salt, pepper and lemon juice. Add lemon rind, scallions and tomato slices and cover with breadcrumbs, sprinkle with grated cheese and dot with butter. Cover and cook in a moderate oven for 15 minutes, remove lid and cook a further 15 minutes until top is golden brown.

# Smoked Haddock Pie

Serves: 4
Cooking time: 35 minutes
Oven: 200°C 400°F

> 1 lb (500 g) smoked haddock
> 1 cup (250 ml) milk
> 2 hard boiled eggs, sliced
> 3 tablespoons butter
> 3 tablespoons flour
> salt and pepper
> 1 lb (500 g) potatoes, cooked and mashed
> 2 tablespoons grated cheese

Arrange fish in a greased pan, add ½ cup of milk, cover and simmer gently for 10 minutes. Drain fish, but reserve the liquid, bone and flake and spoon into a greased oven proof casserole dish and top with egg slices.
Melt butter in a pan, stir in flour and cook until bubbly. Stir in remaining milk with the reserved liquid, season with salt and pepper and, stirring constantly, bring to the boil and pour over fish and eggs. Cover with mashed potatoes and top with grated cheese. Cook in a hot oven for 20 minutes until golden brown.

# Trevally in Beer Batter

Serves: 4
Cooking time: 15–20 minutes

> 1½ lbs (750 g) — fillets of trevally
> 8 tablespoons flour
> 1½ cups (375 ml) flat beer
> salt and pepper
> oil for frying
> chopped parsley
> hot tartare sauce — see recipe page 90

Blend 4 tablespoons flour, salt and pepper with beer until smooth for a batter.
Dredge fish in remaining flour, shake off excess, and dip in batter, drain and dust again with flour, then return to batter and drain.
Heat oil in a pan and slowly lower fish, 1 piece at a time, into the hot oil. Cook on all sides until golden brown and drain on paper towels.
Serve sprinkled with parsley, accompanied by hot tartar sauce.

# Trout and Apples with Lemon Butter Sauce

Serves: 4
Cooking time: 25–30 minutes

4 cleaned trout
4 cooking apples, peeled, cut in rings and cored
¼ cup (65 ml) white wine
salt
·milk
flour
salt and pepper
8 tablespoons butter
2 tablespoons lemon juice
dash of seasoned pepper

Place apple rings in a shallow flameproof casserole dish and pour wine over, cover and cook 5–6 minutes. Uncover and transfer dish to the broiler and cook under high heat for 5–6 minutes to lightly brown the apples. Remove and keep hot. Meanwhile, season trout inside with salt, dip fish in milk, then toss in flour seasoned with salt and pepper. Heat ½ the butter in a pan, add fish and cook to brown on all sides. Remove fish onto apples and keep hot. Add remaining butter to the pan with lemon juice and seasoned pepper and cook for 3–4 minutes.

Serve trout and apple rings with lemon butter sauce.

GRILLED LOBSTER WITH CREAM SAUCE (RECIPE PAGE 62) ▶

# Grilled Lobster with Cream Sauce

Serves:  2
Cooking time:  15–20 minutes

*1½ lbs (750 g) cooked lobster*
*4 tablespoons melted butter*
*salt and pepper*
*juice of 1 lemon*
*1 lemon*
*chopped parsley*

**Sauce:**
*3 scallions, chopped*
*½ cup (125 ml) white wine*
*2 egg yolks*
*¼ cup heavy cream*
*1½ tablespoons butter*
*salt and pepper*
*1 tablespoon brandy*

Split lobster in half lengthways and place on a broiler rack flesh side up and brush liberally with butter. Grill 10 cm (4″) from heat for 5–6 minutes to warm through, baste with more butter and broil a further 4–5 minutes.

Meanwhile for sauce: combine scallions and wine in a pan and boil to reduce to ¼ cup, strain liquid and set aside. Beat egg yolks and cream together in a bowl until smooth.

Melt butter in a pan and stir in egg and cream mixture, salt, pepper, brandy and strained liquid. Heat, stirring briskly until thick and smooth.

Serve lobster garnished with cut lemon and parsley and cream sauce on the side.

*(Illustrated on page 61.)*

# Easy Tuna Casserole

Serves:  4
Cooking time:  30 minutes
Oven:  180°C   350°F

*15¾ oz (450 g) can of tuna (or pink salmon)*
*1 packet cream of chicken soup*
*1 cup (250 ml) milk*
*1 tablespoon chopped parsley*
*1 egg, beaten*
*1 medium onion, sliced thinly*
*1 stalk of celery, chopped*
*boiled rice*

Combine soup mix with a little milk in a pan and stir until smooth, gradually add remainder of the milk, bring to the boil and simmer gently 2–3 minutes. Remove from heat and cool. Stir in egg. Grease an ovenproof casserole dish and arrange onion, celery and tuna. Spoon soup mixture over. Cover and cook in a moderate oven for 25 minutes. Serve over rice, sprinkled with parsley.

# Fish and White Grapes

Serves:  4
Cooking time:  30–35 minutes
Oven:  180°C   350°F

*1½ lbs (750 g) whiting or sole fillets*
*juice of 1 lemon*
*salt and pepper*
*1 teaspoon thyme*
*1 large onion, sliced thinly in rings*
*¼ lb (125 g) white grapes, seeded*
*1 cup (250 ml) white wine*
*½ cup (125 ml) water*
*1½ tablespoons butter*
*1 tablespoon flour*
*1 tablespoon chopped parsley*

Arrange fish in an ovenproof casserole dish, squeeze with lemon juice and sprinkle with salt, pepper and thyme, add onion rings and grapes and pour over wine and water. Cover and cook in a moderate oven for 25 minutes, strain off liquid and reserve and keep fish warm.

Melt butter in a pan, stir in flour and cook 1–2 minutes, gradually stir in reserved liquid and parsley and bring to the boil, stirring constantly, until thick and smooth. Serve fish and grapes with the sauce.

# Sole with Hollandaise Sauce

Serves: 4
Cooking time: 20 minutes

  1½ lbs (750 g) fillets of sole
  1 tablespoon lemon juice
  4 scallions, finely chopped
  1 teaspoon tarragon
  salt and pepper
  ½ cup (125 ml) white wine
  7 oz (220 g) can of spinach
  chopped parsley
  ¼ cup heavy cream
  6 tablespoons hollandaise sauce, heated — see
    recipe page 90

Brush fish with lemon juice and fold over with dark skin inside and arrange in one layer in a flameproof casserole dish. Add scallions, tarragon, salt, pepper and wine, bring to the boil and simmer gently for 7–8 minutes until fish is flaky; remove fish carefully and keep warm.
Drain spinach and add to casserole dish and heat, stirring occasionally; fold in cream and heat. Serve fish with spinach sauce and spoon hollandaise sauce over.

# Fish with Parsley Sauce and Asparagus

Serves: 4
Cooking time: 40–45 minutes
Oven: 180°C 350°F

  1½ lbs (750 g) fillets of mullet
  juice of 1 lemon
  salt and pepper
  ½ cup (125 ml) white wine
  15½ oz (440 g) can of asparagus
  3 tablespoons butter
  1 tablespoon chopped chives
  2 tablespoons chopped parsley
  3 tablespoons flour
  ½ cup (125 ml) milk

Arrange fish fillets in an ovenproof casserole dish, sprinkle with lemon juice, salt and pepper and let stand 20 minutes. Pour wine over fish, cover and cook in a moderate oven for 25 minutes. Drain fish and keep hot, but reserve the liquid.
Heat asparagus, drain off liquid and reserve, keep asparagus hot.
Melt butter in a pan, add chives, salt, pepper and parsley, stir in flour and cook 2–3 minutes; gradually stir in milk, the reserved fish liquid and 2 tablespoons of the asparagus liquid. Bring to the boil, stirring constantly, and simmer for 5 minutes until sauce has thickened.
Serve parsley sauce over fish with asparagus.

# Sweet and Sour Fish

Serves: 4
Cooking time: 30 minutes

  1½ lbs (750 g) fillets of fish
  flour
  1 egg, beaten with a little water
  dry breadcrumbs
  oil for frying
  3 tablespoons brown sugar
  ½ cup (125 ml) vinegar
  1 cup (250 ml) pineapple juice
  1½ tablespoons cornstarch
  1 tablespoon soy sauce
  1 tablespoon red wine
  1 medium carrot, grated
  4 scallions, finely chopped
  ¼ lb (125 g) mushrooms, chopped

Dredge fish fillets in flour, dip in egg and toss in breadcrumbs to coat. Heat oil in a pan, add fish and cook, turning often, until golden brown. Remove fish and keep warm.
Mix brown sugar, vinegar and pineapple juice in an enamel or glass pan, heat and simmer for 2–3 minutes to make basic sauce. Blend cornstarch with soy sauce and wine until smooth, then stir into basic sauce. Bring to the boil and, still stirring, add carrots, scallions and mushrooms, reduce heat, cover and simmer gently for 8–10 minutes. Serve sweet and sour sauce over fish.

TROUT AND HAM CASSEROLE (RECIPE OPPOSITE PAGE)

TROUT WITH ALMONDS (RECIPE OPPOSITE PAGE)

# Marinated Spiced Fish

Serves: 4
Cooking time: 45 minutes
Oven: 160°C 325°F

1½ lbs (750 g) fish fillets
1 tablespoon lemon juice
dash of mace
dash of allspice
salt and pepper
½ cup (125 ml) wine vinegar
¾ cup (185 ml) white wine
1 small carrot, grated
1 medium onion, minced
bouquet garni
2 extra medium onions, sliced
chopped parsley

Combine lemon juice, mace, allspice, salt, pepper, vinegar and wine in a glass or enamel pan, add carrots, minced onion and bouquet garni. Bring to the boil and simmer gently for 25 minutes. Strain off liquid and reserve.
Line a baking dish with aluminium foil and arrange fish in the base, pour the reserved liquid over the fish and top with sliced onion rings. Cover tightly with foil and cook in a moderately slow oven for 20 minutes. Remove from the oven, cool and chill. Sprinkle with parsley.

# Trout with Almonds

Serves: 4
Cooking time: 30 minutes

4 small trout
salt
flour
8 tablespoons butter
1 tablespoon lemon juice
dash of seasoned pepper
¼ cup (65 ml) cream
½ cup blanched, sliced almonds

Sprinkle fish inside and out with salt and dust with flour. Melt 4 tablespoons of butter in a pan, add fish and cook, turning often, until light golden. Remove fish to a flameproof casserole dish.
To pan juices add remaining 4 tablespoons of butter and melt; stir in lemon juice, seasoned pepper and cream. Heat, stirring constantly, then pour sauce over the fish. Top with blanched almonds and broil 2″ (5 cm) from heat, until top is golden brown.
(Illustrated on opposite page.)

# Trout and Ham Casserole

Serves: 4
Cooking time: 40–45 minutes
Oven: 150°C 300°F

4 cleaned trout
salt
juice of 1 lemon
½ lb (250 g) ham slices
1½ tablespoons butter
4 scallions, finely chopped
¼ lb (125 g) mushrooms, finely chopped
salt and seasoned pepper
½ cup (125 ml) white wine
¼ cup (65 ml) cream

Season trout inside and out with salt and place in a greased ovenproof casserole dish, sprinkle with lemon juice. Arrange ham slices on top of fish.
Melt butter in a pan, add scallions and mushrooms and sauté 3–4 minutes; stir in salt, seasoned pepper and wine and bring to the boil, stirring; remove from heat and fold in the cream. Spoon mixture over the fish, cover and cook in a slow oven for 30 minutes.
Serve trout and ham with creamy scallions and mushrooms.
(Illustrated on opposite page.)

# Savoury Cod Steaks

Serves: 4
Cooking time: 25 minutes

*4 cod steaks*
*½ cup (125 ml) milk*
*3 tablespoons butter*
*2 large onions, sliced*
*1 clove garlic, crushed*
*salt and pepper*
*3 tablespoons tomato purée*
*1 teaspoon paprika*
*½ cup (125 ml) red wine*
*lemon wedges*
*chopped parsley*
*4 black olives*

Place the fish steaks in a flame proof casserole dish, pour the milk over, cover and simmer for 10 minutes; drain and keep fish warm.
Melt the butter in a pan, add onions and garlic and sauté until transparent, season with salt and pepper. Stir in tomato purée, paprika and red wine and cook gently, stirring constantly, for 10 minutes.
Serve sauce over cod steaks, sprinkle with parsley and top with an olive; serve lemon wedges on the side.

NEST OF SCALLOPS (RECIPE PAGE 68)

FRIED SOLE WITH PARSLEY POTATOES (RECIPE PAGE 68)

# Fried Sole with Parsley Potatoes

Serves: 4
Cooking time: 12–15 minutes

1½ lbs (750 g) fillets of sole
juice of 1 lemon
flour
1 egg beaten with a little water
dry breadcrumbs
2 cups hot mashed potatoes
3 tablespoons chopped parsley
1 tablespoon cream
lemon wedges
radishes

Place fish on a plate, drizzle lemon juice over and let stand 10 minutes. Drain fish, dredge in flour, dip in milk and toss in breadcrumbs.
Heat oil in a pan, add fish and cook on all sides until golden brown. Drain on paper towels and keep warm.
Whip potatoes, parsley and cream together and serve with the fish, garnished with lemon wedges and radishes.
*(Illustrated on page 67.)*

# Sole in Easy Mushroom Sauce

Serves: 4
Cooking time: 15 minutes

1½ lbs (750 g) fillets of sole
1 packet mushroom soup
1 teaspoon thyme
dash of oregano
dash of sweet basil
dash of marjoram
¼ cup (65 ml) white wine
1 cup (250 ml) sour cream
3 tablespoons butter
salt and pepper
chopped parsley

In a bowl combine soup powder, thyme, oregano, sweet basil and marjoram with the wine until smooth and fold in sour cream.
Melt butter in a pan over low heat, then arrange fish fillets in the pan, sprinkle with salt and pepper and pour soup mixture over the fish. Cover tightly and bring to the boil, reduce heat and simmer gently for 10–12 minutes. Sprinkle with parsley at serving.

# Nest of Scallops

Serves: 4
Cooking time: 35–40 minutes
Oven: 190°C 375°F

1 lb (500 g) scallops
¾ cup (185 ml) white wine
¾ cup (185 ml) water
2 cups fluffy mashed potatoes
1 packet frozen spinach, thawed
4 tablespoons butter
5 tablespoons flour
½ cup (125 ml) hot milk
salt and pepper
4 tablespoons grated cheese

Wash and dry scallops and place them in a pan with wine and water; bring to the boil, reduce heat, cover and simmer gently for 4–5 minutes. Remove scallops and set aside. Boil liquid briskly to reduce to ½ cup, remove from heat and reserve.
Grease an oven tray and on it pipe mashed potatoes in thick 4″ (10 cm) discs; pipe thickly around edge of each disc to make potato cases. Spoon spinach into base of potato cases and spoon scallops on top.
Make mornay sauce by melting butter in a pan, stir in flour and cook 1–2 minutes, gradually stir in reserved liquid and hot milk and cook, stirring constantly, until thick and smooth. Remove from heat, season with salt and pepper and fold in cheese and stir until cheese melts. Spoon mornay sauce over scallops in potato cases. Cook in a pre-heated moderately hot oven 10–12 minutes until light brown. Serve immediately.
*(Illustrated on page 67.)*

# Sole and Scallions in Creamy Wine Sauce

Serves: 4
Cooking time: 20−25 minutes

*1½ lbs (750 g) fillets of sole*
*4 scallions, finely chopped*
*½ lb (250 g) mushrooms finely sliced*
*2 tablespoons chopped parsley*
*¾ cup (185 ml) white wine*
*1 cup (250 ml) heavy cream*
*salt and pepper*

In a flameproof casserole dish, place scallions, mushrooms and ½ the parsley, arrange fish on top and pour wine over; cover and bring to the boil, lower heat and simmer gently for 5 minutes. Strain off liquid into a pan and boil to reduce quantity by half, stir in cream, salt and pepper until smooth, heat, but do not boil. Serve sauce over fish and sprinkle with remaining parsley.

# Sole in Creamy Mushroom Sauce

Serves: 4
Cooking time: 40 minutes
Oven: 180°C 350°F

*1½ lbs (750 g) fillets of sole*
*salt and pepper*
*4 spring onions, sliced, including tops*
*1 lemon, thinly sliced*
*¾ cup (185 ml) white wine*
*water*
*3 tablespoons butter*
*¼ lb (125 g) button mushrooms, sliced*
*1½ tablespoons flour*
*2 egg yolks*
*¼ cup (65 ml) cream*
*chopped parsley*

Season fish fillets with salt and pepper, fold over and arrange in a greased ovenproof casserole dish, spread fish with onions and lemon slices and add wine. Cover tightly and cook in a moderate oven for 25 minutes; remove dish from oven, discard lemon slices and strain liquid into a measuring cup, add water to make 1 cup (250 ml); keep fish warm.

Melt butter in a pan, add mushrooms and sauté gently for 3 minutes, remove mushrooms and set aside, stir in flour and cook 1−2 minutes, gradually stir in reserved liquid and bring to the boil, stirring constantly. Return mushrooms to sauce and remove pan from heat.

In a bowl beat egg yolks and cream together, add a little of the sauce, still beating, then stir mixture into the sauce. Return to heat and simmer gently for 1−2 minutes, stirring constantly. Serve sauce over fish and sprinkle with parsley.

# Sole in Mornay Sauce

Serves: 4
Cooking time: 35 minutes
Oven: 190°C 375°F

*1½ lbs (750 g) fillets of sole*
*salt and pepper*
*1 small onion, finely chopped*
*1 bay leaf*
*½ cup (125 ml) white wine*
*½ cup (125 ml) water*
*3 tablespoons butter*
*3 tablespoons flour*
*½ cup (125 ml) milk*
*¾ cup grated cheese*

Arrange fish fillets in an ovenproof casserole dish, season with salt and pepper, add onion, bay leaf, wine and water. Cover and bring to the boil and simmer for 5 minutes; strain off liquid and reserve ¾ cup (185 ml) and discard bay leaf. Melt butter in a pan, stir in flour and cook, stirring, until bubbly. Gradually stir in reserved liquid and milk and bring to the boil, stirring constantly, until thick and smooth. Fold in 2 tablespoons of cheese and pour sauce over the fish, top with remaining cheese. Cook in a moderately hot oven for 15 minutes until golden brown.

# Scallops and Mussels in Breadcrumbs

Serves:  4–6
Cooking time:  35–40 minutes
Oven:  190°C  375°F

½ lb (250 g) scallops
½ lb (250 g) mussels
8 tablespoons butter
2 medium onions, finely chopped
1 clove garlic, crushed
1 cup (250 ml) white wine
bouquet garni
salt and pepper
1 ½ cups soft bread, diced
dry breadcrumbs
chopped parsley
scallop shells or individual ovenproof dishes

Remove corals from scallops, chop them finely and reserve. Melt 4 tablespoons of butter in a pan, add onions and sauté until soft, add garlic and chopped corals, cover and simmer gently for 10 minutes. Add wine, bouquet garni, salt, pepper, scallops and mussels, cover and cook gently for 10 minutes. Remove from heat, discard bouquet garni and fold in soft breadcrumbs to absorb most of the liquid. Spoon mixture into shells and sprinkle with dry breadcrumbs, dot with remaining 1 tablespoon of butter and cook in a pre-heated moderately hot oven for 8–10 minutes until tops are golden brown. Serve sprinkled with chopped parsley.

FISH FINGERS, RICE & PINEAPPLE (RECIPE PAGE 72)

CRUMBED FISH WITH LEMON BUTTER SAUCE (RECIPE PAGE 72)

# Crumbed Fish with Lemon Butter Sauce

Serves:  4
Cooking time:   15 minutes

*1½ lbs (750 g) fish fillets*
*flour*
*salt and pepper*
*1 egg, beaten with a little water*
*dry breadcrumbs*
*3 tablespoons oil*
*1½ tablespoons butter*
*lemon wedges*
*parsley*
*lemon butter sauce — see recipe page 89*

Roll fish in flour seasoned with salt and pepper, dip in egg and toss in breadcrumbs to coat. Heat oil and butter in a pan, add fish and cook quickly on all sides until golden brown, drain on paper towels and keep warm.
Serve fish with lemon butter sauce, garnished with lemon wedges and parsley.
*(Illustrated on page 71.)*

# Fish Fingers, Rice and Pineapple

Serves:  4
Cooking time:   20–25 minutes

*12 frozen fish fingers*
*1½ tablespoons butter*
*1½ tablespoons oil*
*15¾ oz (450 g) can pineapple rings in syrup*
*1 tablespoon cider vinegar*
*¼ cup golden raisins*
*salt and pepper*
*2 cups boiled rice*

Heat butter and oil in a pan, add fish fingers and cook until golden brown all over, remove fish and keep warm. Add drained pineapple rings to pan juices and heat through, remove and keep warm. To the pan juices stir in pineapple syrup, cider vinegar, raisins, salt, pepper and rice and heat, stirring constantly, until piping hot.
Serve rice mixture topped with fish fingers and pineapple rings.
*(Illustrated on page 71.)*

# Mushroom Filled Sole

Serves:  4
Cooking time:   45–50 minutes
Oven:   180°C   350°F

*1½ lbs (750 g) — 8 fillets of sole*
*4 tablespoons butter*
*1 large onion, finely chopped*
*½ lb (250 g) mushrooms, sliced thinly*
*3 tablespoons chopped parsley*
*salt and pepper*
*½ cup (125 ml) white wine*
*1½ tablespoons flour*
*½ cup (125 ml) heavy cream*
*1 teaspoon paprika*

Melt 2 tablespoons butter in a pan, add onion and sauté until transparent, add mushrooms and ½ the parsley and sauté 8–10 minutes, stirring occasionally.
Arrange 4 of the fish fillets in the base of a greased ovenproof casserole, spoon over the sauteed mixture and arrange the remaining 4 fillets on top; season with salt and pepper, pour wine over fish and dot with remaining butter. Cover and cook in a moderate oven for 15 minutes, remove dish from oven, strain off liquid and reserve.
Blend flour and cream together in a pan, stir in reserved liquid and cook gently, stirring constantly, until thickened and pour over fish. Return dish to the oven and cook a further 10 minutes. At serving sprinkle with paprika and remaining parsley.

# Grilled Marinated Scallops

Serves:   4
Cooking time:   10–15 minutes

1½ lbs (750 g) scallops
½ teaspoon ground ginger
1 clove garlic, crushed
2 tablespoons lemon juice
6 tablespoons salad oil
4 tablespoons soy sauce
4 tablespoons water

In a blender combine ginger, garlic, lemon juice, salad oil, soy sauce and water and blend until smooth. Place scallops in a bowl and pour mixture over and let stand to marinate for at least 2 hours. Remove scallops, drain and set aside. Pour marinade into a pan and simmer gently for 5 minutes, remove from heat. Thread scallops on skewers and place on a broiling rack. Cook 2" (5 cm) from high heat for about 5 minutes, turning often and brushing with marinade.

# Fish Fillets in Cheese Sauce

Serves:   4
Cooking time:   30 minutes
Oven:   180°C   350°F

1½ lbs (750 g) of fish fillets
6 tablespoons butter
2 tablespoons lemon juice
3 tablespoons flour
salt and pepper
1 cup (250 ml) milk
3 tablespoons grated cheese

Melt 2 tablespoons of butter in an ovenproof casserole dish and stir in lemon juice, add fish fillets and cook, basting, for 4–5 minutes. Set aside. Melt 2 tablespoons of butter in a pan, stir in flour, salt and pepper and cook, stirring, until bubbly, gradually stir in milk and bring to the boil, stirring constantly. Remove from heat and fold in 2 tablespoons cheese. Pour cheese sauce over fish, sprinkle with remaining cheese and dot with remaining butter. Cook in a pre-heated moderate oven 10–12 minutes until top is browned.

# Fish Fillets and Shrimp

Serves:   4
Cooking time:   35 minutes

1 lb (500 g) fish fillets
½ lb (250 g) shelled and de-veined shrimp
4 cups (1 liter) of water
1 teaspoon salt
3 tablespoon butter
1 large onion, chopped
½ lb (250) tomatoes, peeled and chopped
3 tablespoons flour
salt and pepper
½ cup (125 ml) white wine
¾ cup (185 ml) water
1 cup cooked, diced potatoes
8 oz (220 g) can corn, drained
½ cup (125 ml) heavy cream
chopped parsley

Place fish fillets in a pan with water and salt and simmer gently for 5–6 minutes. Remove fish carefully and place in a flameproof casserole dish and add shrimp.
Melt 1 tablespoon of butter in a pan, add onion and sauté until soft, add tomatoes and cook 6–7 minutes. Remove onion and tomatoes onto fish. Add remaining butter to pan juices and melt, stir in flour, salt and pepper and cook until bubbly, gradually stir in wine and water and bring to the boil, stirring constantly. Add potatoes and corn and stir. Pour mixture over fish and shrimp, cover and simmer gently for 10 minutes. Fold in cream and heat, but do not boil. Serve sprinkled with parsley.

# Lobster in Batter

Serves: 6
Cooking time: 10–12 minutes

   3 lbs (1½ kg) cooked lobster
   juice of 1 lemon
   ½ cup flour
   ½ cup (125 ml) milk
   1 egg
   salt and pepper
   oil and frying
   ½ cup prepared mayonnaise
   2 tablespoons chopped chives

Remove the meat in pieces from the lobster and place in a bowl, squeeze over lemon juice and let stand 10 minutes. Beat flour and milk together until smooth, add egg, salt and pepper and beat to a smooth thick batter. Drain the lobster carefully and dip pieces into the batter to completely coat.
Heat oil in a deep pan until hot, add lobster pieces a few at a time and cook for 5–6 minutes until golden brown. Drain on paper towels.
Combine mayonnaise and chives and serve with lobster.

COD FILLETS IN CHIVE CREAM SAUCE (RECIPE PAGE 76) ▶

# Cod Fillets in Chive Cream Sauce

Serves: 4
Cooking time: 20–25 minutes

1 ½ lbs (750 g) cod fillets
1 cup (250 ml) white wine
¾ cup (185 ml) water
1 large onion, chopped
1 medium carrot, chopped
1 teaspoon thyme
1 bay leaf
sprig of parsley
salt and pepper
2 tablespoons chopped chives
3 eggs, beaten
¼ cup (65 ml) heavy cream

Combine wine, water, onion, carrot, thyme, bay leaf, parsley, salt and pepper in a deep pan, bring to the boil and simmer gently for 30 minutes; strain and reserve liquid. Place fish fillets in a flameproof casserole dish and add the reserved liquid. Cover and cook gently for 30 minutes. Remove and drain fish and keep warm. Boil liquid to reduce by half; lower heat and add chives. Combine eggs and cream and fold into the liquid, stirring briskly. Heat until thick and smooth, but do not boil. Serve sauce over fillets.
*(Illustrated on page 75.)*

# Lobster Mornay

Serves: 2
Cooking time: 15–20 minutes

1 cooked lobster, split in half
4 tablespoons butter
3 tablespoons flour
1 cup (250 ml) milk
salt
dash of cayenne pepper
½ cup grated cheese
½ cup (125 ml) heavy cream
chopped parsley
boiled rice

Remove lobster meat from the shell and claws and set aside. Place shells on a broiling tray.
Melt 2 tablespoons butter in a pan, stir in flour and cook, stirring, until bubbly. Gradually stir in milk and bring to the boil, stirring constantly. Remove from heat and fold in ½ the cheese, all the cream, and the lobster meat. Spoon mixture into lobster shells, sprinkle with the remaining cheese and dot with remaining butter. Place under pre-heated broiler and cook 8–9 minutes to brown.
Serve lobster mornay on a bed of rice.

# Lobster Newburg

Serves: 4
Cooking time: 20 minutes

3 lbs (1 ½ kg) — 2 cooked lobsters
6 tablespoons butter
¼ cup (65 ml) brandy
½ cup (125 ml) dry sherry
½ cup (125 ml) heavy cream
2 egg yolks, beaten
salt and pepper
boiled rice
chopped parsley

Cut lobsters in half, scoop out meat and dice; warm the shells.
Melt butter in a pan, add lobster meat and sauté until coated with butter, 2–3 minutes. Stir in brandy and sherry and simmer for 5 minutes, fold in half the cream and keep mixture warm. Combine remainder of the cream and egg yolks in a bowl and blend. Then fold into lobster mixture, season with salt and pepper and heat, stirring constantly.
Spoon lobster mixture into the shells, sprinkle with parsley and serve with hot, boiled rice.

# Lobster Thermidor

Serves:  4
Cooking time:   40–45 minutes

3 lbs (1 ½ kg) — 2 cooked lobsters
1 large onion, finely chopped
6 cloves
1 bay leaf
1 cup (250 ml) milk
6 tablespoons butter
3 tablespoons flour
salt and seasoned pepper
½ teaspoon prepared mustard
3 scallions, finely chopped
½ cup (125 ml) white wine
1 cup (250 ml) cream
½ cup grated cheese

Cut lobsters in half, remove meat and dice, reserve shells. Combine onion, cloves, bay leaf and milk in a pan, heat and simmer for 7–8 minutes; strain and reserve liquid.
Melt 2 tablespoons of butter in a pan, stir in flour, salt, pepper and mustard and cook 1–2 minutes, gradually stir in reserved liquid and cook, still stirring, until the sauce thickens, then set aside.
Melt remaining 2 tablespoons of butter in a pan, add scallions and sauté 2–3 minutes until soft. Stir in wine and cook over high heat to reduce liquid to ¼ cup; stir in sauce and simmer gently for 5 minutes. Fold in the cream and ⅔ of the cheese until smooth, add lobster meat and heat through over low heat.
Spoon mixture into lobster shells, sprinkle with remaining cheese and broil under high heat until golden brown.

# Macaroni Cheese Fish

Serves:  4
Cooking time:   30 minutes
Oven:   180°C   350°F

1 lb (500 g) fish fillets, diced
juice of 1 lemon
salt and pepper
1 ½ tablespoons butter
1 medium onion, chopped
1 ½ tablespoons flour
1 cup (250 ml) milk
3 tablespoons grated cheese
2 cups cooked macaroni

Place diced fish in an ovenproof casserole dish, sprinkle with lemon juice, salt and pepper and let stand for 30 minutes, drain off liquid and reserve. Melt butter in a pan, add onion and sauté until transparent, stir in flour and cook 1–2 minutes. Gradually stir in reserved liquid and milk and bring to the boil, stirring constantly. Fold in ½ the cheese and stir until melted and sauce has thickened. Spoon macaroni over fish, add sauce and top with remainder of the cheese. Cook in a moderate oven 25 minutes until golden brown.

# Mornay Cod Fillets

Serves:  4
Cooking time:   30 minutes
Oven:   180°C   350°F

1 ½ lbs (750 g) cod fillets
2 tablespoons lemon juice
salt and pepper
3 tablespoons butter
1 large onion, finely chopped
1 ½ tablespoons flour
2 tablespoons grated cheese
1 tablespoon tomato catsup
1 teaspoon Worcestershire sauce
1 cup (250 ml) milk
3 tablespoons dry breadcrumbs
chopped parsley

Sprinkle lemon juice, salt and pepper over the fish and arrange fillets in a greased ovenproof casserole dish and let stand 20 minutes.
Melt 1 tablespoon of butter in a pan, add onion and sauté until golden, stir in flour and half the cheese and cook 1–2 minutes. Stir in the 2 sauces and the milk and bring to the boil, stirring constantly, and simmer until thick and smooth. Pour sauce over the fish, top with breadcrumbs and remaining cheese and dot with remaining butter. Cook in a moderate oven for 25 minutes until top is golden brown. Sprinkle with parsley at serving.

# Mussels with Saffron Sauce

Serves: 4
Cooking time: 15 minutes

36 mussels
1 cup (250 ml) white wine
1 medium onion, chopped
4 tablespoons butter

**Sauce:**
2 teaspoons saffron powder
4 tablespoons butter
1½ tablespoons flour
4 eggs, beaten

Scrub mussels under running water.

Melt butter in a flameproof casserole, add onion, wine and mussels. Cover and cook 5–6 minutes until shells open. Remove one half of the shell from each mussel; trim off the beard and arrange mussels on a serving dish. Reserve liquid.

For sauce: melt butter in a pan, stir in saffron and flour and cook until bubbly. Stir in reserved liquid and fold in beaten eggs. Heat, stirring constantly, until sauce is thick and smooth. Spoon over the mussels.

# Seafood and Mushrooms

Serves:   4
Cooking time:   40 minutes
Oven:   180°C   350°F

*1½ lbs (750 g) — 4 pieces of sole, filleted*
*¼ lb (125 g) shelled and de-veined shrimp*
*6 oz (190 g) can button mushrooms*
*2 tablespoons lemon juice*
*3 tablespoons chopped parsley*
*1½ tablespoons oil*
*2 tablespoons brandy*
*½ cup (125 ml) white wine*
*1½ tablespoons butter*
*1½ tablespoons flour*

Sprinkle sole fillets with lemon juice, salt, pepper and 2 tablespoons of parsley, roll each fillet and fasten with a toothpick. Arrange fish rolls in a greased ovenproof casserole dish, brush with oil and sprinkle with brandy. Add mushrooms with liquid, shrimp and wine. Cover tightly with aluminium foil to seal and cook in a moderate oven for 25 minutes. Strain off liquid and reserve.

Melt butter in a pan, stir in flour and cook 2 minutes, add remaining 1 tablespoon parsley. Gradually stir in reserved liquid and bring to the boil, stirring constantly, until sauce thickens. Spoon sauce over seafood and mushrooms and return to oven for 5 minutes.

# Smoked Haddock with Anchovy Sauce

Serves:  4
Cooking time:  10 minutes

  1½ lbs (750 g) smoked haddock cut in 4 pieces
  water
  1½ tablespoons butter
  paprika

  **Sauce:**
  1 tablespoon anchovy paste
  dash cayenne pepper
  ½ teaspoon prepared mustard
  salt
  1 teaspoon lemon juice
  1 teaspoon Worcestershire sauce
  ¼ cup (65 ml) sour cream

Place fish in a pan and cover with cold water, bring to the boil and simmer 2 minutes, drain and keep warm.
For the sauce: combine anchovy paste in a pan with cayenne pepper, mustard, salt, lemon juice and Worcestershire sauce; fold in sour cream and heat.
To serve smoked haddock dot with butter, sprinkle with paprika, add sauce on the side.

# Sole à là Lorraine

Serves:  4
Cooking time:  30–35 minutes

  1½ lbs (750 g) — 4 small sole
  4 tablespoons butter
  flour
  salt and pepper
  1 small onion, finely chopped
  3 scallions, finely chopped
  2 large tomatoes, peeled and chopped
  ½ cup (125 ml) concentrated fish stock — see
    recipe page 89
  ¾ cup (185 ml) white wine
  1 tablespoon chopped parsley
  6 tablespoons heavy cream

Dredge fish in flour seasoned with salt and pepper. Melt butter in a pan, add fish and cook on both sides until lightly browned. Remove from pan and keep hot.
To pan juices add onion and scallions and sauté until soft, add tomatoes and cook, stirring, to pulp. Stir in stock, wine and parsley and bring to the boil, reduce heat and simmer 8–10 minutes, stirring constantly. Fold in cream and heat, but do not boil, and serve over the fish.

# Sole and Salmon Rolls

Serves:  4
Cooking time:  40 minutes
Oven:  180°C  350°F

  1½ lbs (750 g) fillets of sole
  8 oz (220 g) can pink salmon, drained and flaked
  salt and pepper
  3 scallions, finely chopped
  1 cup (250 ml) white wine
  1 cup (250 ml) hot water
  2 tablespoons butter
  3 tablespoons flour
  1 tablespoon lemon juice
  ¼ cup (65 ml) heavy cream
  chopped parsley

Place some of the salmon on each fish fillet, season with salt and pepper, wrap fish over salmon and fasten with toothpicks to make rolls. Arrange rolls in a greased ovenproof casserole dish, spread scallions evenly on top and add wine and hot water. Cover tightly and cook in a moderate oven for 30 minutes. Remove rolls carefully and keep warm, reserve stock. Melt butter in a pan, add flour and cook, stirring, 1–2 minutes, gradually stir in reserved stock and lemon juice and bring to the boil, stirring constantly, and cook until sauce thickens. Fold in cream, heat, but do not boil. Serve sauce over fish rolls and sprinkle with parsley.

# Sole with Avocado and Nuts

Serves:   4
Cooking time:   15 minutes

 1½ lbs (750 g) of sole fillets
 4 tablespoons lemon juice
 salt and pepper
 1 avocado, peeled, seeded and chopped
 flour
 4 tablespoons butter or margarine
 ¼ cup chopped Macadamia nuts, warmed

Arrange fish fillets in a glass dish and sprinkle with 1 tablespoon lemon juice, salt and pepper and let stand 20 minutes, drain off liquid and reserve and dredge fish in flour. Sprinkle 1 tablespoon of lemon juice over avocado to prevent browning.
Melt butter in a pan, add fish and cook 7–8 minutes until golden brown, turning often. Remove fish and keep warm. Add reserved liquid to pan juices and bring to the boil, stir in parsley and avocado and simmer 2–3 minutes. Serve fish with avocado and sauce and sprinkle with warm Macadamia nuts.

# Grilled Bream

Serves:   4
Cooking time:   15 minutes

 2 lbs (1 kg) — 4 bream
 6 tablespoons butter, melted
 salt and pepper
 chopped parsley

Brush fish inside and out with butter and season with salt and pepper. Arrange fish on a foil lined broiler tray and cook 2″ (5 cm) from heat for 7 minutes each side.
Sprinkle with parsley and serve with tarragon or parsley sauce — see recipe page 90.

# Squid in Chinese Sauce

Serves:   4
Cooking time:   40–45 minutes

 1½ lbs (750 g) squid
 4 tablespoons butter
 3 tablespoons oil
 1 large onion, chopped in large pieces
 1 clove garlic, crushed
 2 scallions, chopped
 1 large carrot, sliced
 1 stalk celery, chopped
 1 teaspoon grated green ginger
 salt and pepper
 3 tablespoons white wine
 1½ tablespoons cornstarch
 1 teaspoon brown sugar
 ¾ cup (185 ml) concentrated fish stock — see
   recipe page 89
 ¼ cup red wine
 2 tablespoons oyster sauce
 4 teaspoons soy sauce
 chopped parsley

Prepare the squid by grasping the head firmly with one hand and gently pulling. The head and inside of body will come away. Remove the bone; wash fish under running cold water and rub off skin. Slice fish down the center and lay pieces out flat with flesh side up; lightly score flesh in a criss cross pattern to help tenderize.
Heat 1 tablespoon of butter and the oil in a pan, add the squid pieces and cook until flesh curls. Remove from pan and drain on paper towels; set aside.
To pan juices add the remaining butter and melt. Add onion, garlic and scallions and sauté until soft; add carrots, celery, ginger, salt, pepper and white wine. Cover and braize over medium heat for 10–12 minutes, shaking pan frequently to avoid burning.
In a bowl mix cornstarch and sugar with a little stock until smooth. Gradually stir in the remaining stock, red wine, oyster and soy sauces and mix well. Stir mixture over the vegetables and cook, stirring constantly, until boiling. Return squid to the pan and heat through, basting with the sauce. Serve sprinkled with parsley.

# Fish Cakes

Serves:  4
Cooking time:  15 minutes

   *1 lb (500 g) fish fillets*
   *1 cup (250 ml) court-bouillon — see recipe page*
     *88*
   *1 cup mashed potatoes*
   *1 teaspoon lemon juice*
   *1 tablespoon chopped parsley*
   *salt and pepper*
   *1½ tablespoons milk*
   *flour*
   *1 egg, beaten with a little water*
   *dry breadcrumbs*
   *oil for frying*
   *hot tartare sauce — see recipe page 90*

Place fish fillets in a pan with court-bouillon and simmer 7–8 minutes, remove fish and flake. Combine fish with potatoes, lemon juice, parsley, salt, pepper and milk and mix well. Shape into 8 cakes, dust with flour, dip in egg and toss in breadcrumbs. Heat oil in a pan until hot, gradually lower fish cakes into oil, 1 at a time and cook, turning often, until golden brown on all sides. Remove cakes and serve hot with hot tartare sauce.

# Sole with Wine Sauce

Serves:  4
Cooking time:  30–35 minutes
Oven:  180°C  350°F

   *1½ lbs (750 g) fillets of lemon sole*
   *juice of 1 lemon*
   *salt and pepper*
   *1 teaspoon thyme*
   *½ teaspoon tarragon*
   *2 tablespoons chopped parsley*
   *1 cup (250 ml) white wine*
   *1½ tablespoons butter*
   *2 scallions, chopped finely*
   *1 small onion, chopped finely*
   *1 tablespoon flour*

Arrange fish fillets in a greased ovenproof casserole dish and sprinkle with lemon juice, salt, pepper, thyme, tarragon, ½ the parsley and pour ½ the wine over. Cover and cook in a moderate oven for 25 minutes. Strain off the liquid and reserve and keep fish warm.
Melt butter in a pan, add scallions and onion and sauté until soft, stir in flour and cook 1–2 minutes, gradually stir in reserved liquid and remaining wine and bring to the boil, stirring constantly, until thick and smooth. Serve wine sauce over fish and sprinkle with remaining parsley.

# Fish Layer Pie

Serves:  4
Cooking time:  35 minutes
Oven:  180°C  350°F

   *1 lb (500 g) fish fillets, diced*
   *4 tablespoons butter*
   *1 large onion, finely chopped*
   *2 cups soft breadcrumbs*
   *¾ lb (375 g) tomatoes, peeled and sliced*
   *1 teaspoon curry powder*
   *salt and pepper*
   *½ cup (125 ml) white wine*

Melt 1 tablespoon of butter in a pan, add onion and sauté until soft.
Place ⅓ of the breadcrumbs in the base of a greased ovenproof casserole dish, add ½ the cooked onion, ½ the tomato slices, sprinkled with curry powder, salt and pepper and add a layer of fish. Cover with layers of ⅓ breadcrumbs, onion, tomato, seasoning and fish. Top with remaining breadcrumbs, pour wine over and dot with remaining butter. Cook in a moderate oven for 30 minutes.

# Tuna and Rice

Serves: 4
Cooking time: 40–45 minutes

15¾ oz (450 g) can tuna, drained and flaked
3 tablespoons butter
1 medium onion, finely chopped
1 stalk of celery, finely chopped
¼ lb (125 g) mushrooms, sliced
2 large tomatoes, peeled and chopped
1 cup (250 ml) concentrated fish stock — see
    recipe page 89
1 cup boiled rice
½ cup (125 ml) cream
1 teaspoon chopped parsley

Melt butter in a pan, add onion and sauté until soft, add celery, mushrooms and tomatoes and cook, stirring, for 5 minutes. Add stock gradually and bring to the boil, reduce heat, cover and simmer for 25 minutes. Fold in tuna and rice and simmer gently a further 2–3 minutes to heat through. Fold in cream and parsley and heat, but do not boil.

# Squid with Shrimp

Serves: 4
Cooking time: 15 minutes

1½ lbs (750 g) squid
½ lb (250 g) fresh shrimp
6 tablespoons butter
2 cloves garlic, crushed
2 tablespoons chopped parsley
salt and pepper

Spread squid pieces flat, inside flesh up, and score with a sharp knife in a diamond pattern to help tenderize. Shell and de-vein the shrimp. On each piece of squid lay a shrimp and lightly wrap and fasten with a toothpick.
Heat butter in a pan, add garlic and half the parsley and stir, add the squid rolls and cook, turning to coat with garlic butter, until shrimp have become pink and the squid has curled. At serving remove the toothpicks and sprinkle squid rolls with remaining parsley. Serve as appetiser or on boiled rice.

# Sole on Stuffed Eggplant

Serves: 4
Cooking time: 50–55 minutes

4 small sole, filleted
2 medium eggplants
salt and pepper
4 tablespoons butter
1 medium onion, finely chopped
2 large tomatoes, peeled and coarsely chopped
1 clove garlic, crushed with ½ teaspoon salt
1 teaspoon basil
dash of thyme
6 tablespoons oil
flour
2 teaspoons lemon juice

Prepare eggplant by cutting in half lengthways, cut around edges and criss cross the center, sprinkle with salt and set aside for 30 minutes. Melt 1 tablespoon of butter in a pan, add onion and cook until golden, add tomatoes and garlic, bring to the boil, stirring, reduce heat, cover and simmer until pulpy, about 18–20 minutes. Stir in basil, thyme, salt and pepper, cover and set aside.
Drain and dry eggplant. Heat oil in a pan until hot, add eggplant, cut side down, and cook until golden brown, turn and lightly cook. Remove eggplant and drain. Scoop out the flesh, chop and fold into the tomato mixture. Heat and simmer 3–4 minutes, then heap the mixture back into the eggplant cases and keep warm.
Dust fish with flour seasoned with salt and pepper. Heat 1 tablespoon of butter in a pan, add fish, skin side up, and cook until golden brown on each side, turning only once. Lift out fish and keep warm. Add remaining 1 tablespoon butter to the pan and heat until light brown, add lemon juice and swirl pan. Serve eggplant with fish on top and pour the lemon butter over them.

# Mackerel with Sautéed Tomatoes

Serves: 4
Cooking time: 20–25 minutes

*4 filleted mackerel*
*flour*
*salt and pepper*
*6 tablespoons butter*
*½ lb (250 g) button mushrooms*
*1 medium onion, chopped*
*1 clove garlic, crushed*
*1 tablespoon wine vinegar*
*3 medium tomatoes, peeled and sliced*
*1 tablespoon chopped chives*
*chopped parsley*

Dust fish with flour seasoned with salt and pepper. Heat 2 tablespoons of butter in a pan; when hot add fish and cook, turning often, until brown and crisp. Remove fish and keep warm, discard pan juices and wipe pan clean. Add 1 tablespoon of butter to the pan and heat, add mushrooms, onion and garlic and sauté 5–6 minutes, sprinkle with salt, pepper, add wine vinegar and cook 1–2 minutes, for a sauce. Meanwhile, heat remaining butter in a pan, add tomato slices and chives and sauté 4–5 minutes. Pour sauce over fish and serve with sautéed tomatoes; sprinkle with parsley.

# Grilled Red Mullet

Serves: 4
Cooking time: 12–15 minutes

*4 small red mullet*
*olive or salad oil*
*3 tablespoons butter*
*3 tablespoons chopped parsley*
*squeeze of lemon juice*
*dash of cayenne*
*1 clove garlic, cut in half*
*salt and pepper*
*lemon wedges*

Scale the mullet and remove the gills and brush well with oil. Place on a broiler tray and cook 5–6 minutes each side.
Meanwhile, combine butter and parsley in a bowl, using a spatula or flat of a knife, add lemon juice and cayenne and mix well. Serve the red mullet rubbed over well with cut garlic, spread with parsley butter, with lemon wedges on the side.

# Sole in Cider Sauce

Serves: 4
Cooking time: 30–35 minutes

*4 fillets of sole*
*1 scallion, chopped*
*1 bay leaf*
*¾ cup (185 ml) cider*
*⅓ cup (85 ml) water*
*concentrated fish stock — see recipe page 89*
*1½ tablespoons butter*
*1½ tablespoons flour*
*2 teaspoons chopped parsley*
*salt and pepper*

Place the fish in a pan with scallion and bay leaf and pour cider and water over. Poach for 20–25 minutes. Strain the liquid from the sole and measure, then add stock to make 1¼ cups (300 ml) and reserve. Discard bay leaf and keep fish warm.
To make Sauce: Melt butter in a pan, add flour and cook, stirring, until bubbly. Gradually stir in reserved liquid and bring to the boil, stirring constantly, and simmer 5–6 minutes, add parsley, salt and pepper to taste and serve over the fillets of sole.

# Fried Whitebait

Serves: 4
Cooking time: 20 minutes

*1½ lbs (750 g) whitebait*
*flour*
*salt and pepper*
*oil for frying*
*lemon wedges*

Toss fish in flour seasoned with salt and pepper. Place ⅓ of the fish in a fry basket. Heat oil in a deep pan to hot, lower in the basket and cook fish for 2−3 minutes. Drain and turn fish onto paper towels. Repeat process until all the fish are lightly cooked. Reheat oil to hot, place all the fish in he basket and lower into the oil, cook for 1−2 minutes, until crisp. Drain well and serve piping hot with lemon wedges.

For added taste dust the cooked fish with a mixture of cayenne pepper, seasoned pepper and salt.

and chervil and cook, covered, for 6−7 minutes, shaking pan occasionally. Drain spinach well and press through a sieve into a bowl and set aside for a purée. Melt 1 tablespoon of butter in a pan, stir in flour and cook 1−2 minutes. Remove pan from heat and stir in hot water, salt, pepper and egg yolk. Return to heat and stir briskly until at the boil. Remove from heat and gradually stir in the remaining 4 tablespoons of butter. Stir in reserved fish liquid, spinach purée and lemon juice and heat, do not boil. Serve fish with green sauce poured over.

# Mackerel with Green Sauce

Serves:  4
Cooking time:   50−55 minutes

*4 filleted mackerel*
*½ cup (125 ml) white wine*
*1 teaspoon chopped tarragon*
*½ teaspoon chervil*
*2 scallions, chopped*

**Green Sauce:**
*2 spinach leaves*
*1 teaspoon chopped tarragon*
*½ teaspoon chervil*
*¼ cup (65 ml) cold water*
*6 tablespoons butter, melted*
*1½ tablespoons flour*
*1 cup (250 ml) hot water*
*salt and pepper*
*2 egg yolks*
*squeeze of lemon juice*

Place the fish in a pan with wine, tarragon and chervil and poach for 15−18 minutes. Remove fish carefully and keep warm. Add scallions to the pan and boil briskly to reduce liquid to a syrupy consistency. Strain and set liquid aside to add to the green sauce.

To make green sauce: rinse spinach under cold water and place in a pan with cold water, tarragon

# Crumbed Whiting and Mushrooms

Serves:  4
Cooking time:   30−35 minutes
Oven:   180°C   350°F

*4 whiting, filleted*
*salt and pepper*
*4 tablespoons butter*
*1 medium onion, finely chopped*
*¼ lb (125 g) mushrooms, finely chopped*
*1½ tablespoons flour*
*1¼ cups (300 ml) concentrated fish stock — see*
   *recipe page 89*
*dash of seasoned pepper*
*½ bay leaf*
*dry breadcrumbs*

Wash and score fish and season with salt and pepper, place in an ovenproof casserole dish. Melt half the butter in a pan, add onion and mushrooms, cover and sweat over low heat for 3−4 minutes. Stir in flour, stock, salt and seasoned pepper and bring to the boil, stirring constantly, and cook 2−3 minutes, add bay leaf, then pour mixture over the fish. Sprinkle top with breadcrumbs and dot with remaining butter. Cook in a moderate oven for 20 minutes, until golden brown. Discard bay leaf at serving.

# Herbed Eel

Serves:  4-6
Cooking time:  25-30 minutes

2 lbs (1 kg) of eel, skinned and washed
4 tablespoons butter
1 large onion, finely chopped
3 tablespoons chopped celery leaves
1 ¼ cups (300 ml) white wine
salt and black pepper
pinch of cloves
pinch of thyme
1 ¼ tablespoons sorrel
½ cup watercress leaves
1 tablespoon chopped parsley
1 tablespoon chervil
pinch sage
½ teaspoon chopped mint
4 egg yolks, beaten
½ cup (125 ml) scalded heavy cream

Melt butter in a pan, add onion and celery. Cut eel into uniform slices and add to the pan, cook over high heat for 7-8 minutes, stirring often. Add wine, salt, black pepper, cloves, thyme, sorrel, watercress, parsley, chervil, sage and mint. Cook for 12-15 minutes, stirring often with a wooden spoon. Remove pan from heat. Combine beaten egg yolks with scalded cream and fold into the pan. Heat and serve. Can be served cold.

# Apple Seasoned Herrings

Serves:  4
Cooking time:  45-50 minutes
Oven:  160°C  325°F

4 herrings, filleted
salt and seasoned pepper
1 medium onion, finely chopped
1 cooking apple, peeled and chopped
1 teaspoon chopped chives
dash of thyme
2 teaspoons chopped parsley
3 tablespoons butter, melted
3 tablespoons cider vinegar

Wash and dry fish and lay open, sprinkle with salt and seasoned pepper. Mix onion, apple, chives, thyme and parsley together and place ¼ of the mixture on each fish. Roll up fish, head to tail. Brush an ovenproof casserole dish with half the butter, put in the herring rolls and spread the remaining butter and the cider vinegar over the fish. Cover and cook in a moderately slow oven for 30 minutes. Remove cover and baste fish, then cook for a further 15-20 minutes.

# Garlic Fish

Serves:  4
Cooking time:  50-55 minutes
Oven:  180°C  350°F

1 ½ lbs (750 g) — 4 cod or flounder steaks
4 tablespoons oil
3 large onions, finely sliced
3 cloves garlic, crushed
1 ½ tablespoons flour
3 teaspoons tomato purée
2 teaspoons paprika
pinch of cayenne
pinch of ground mace
1 ¼ cups (300 ml) red wine
½ cup (125 ml) water
salt and pepper
1 ½ tablespoons butter
¼ cup (65 ml) lemon juice or tarragon vinegar
4 slices bread
oil for frying

Heat 4 tablespoons of oil in a pan, add onions and garlic, cover and sweat over low heat for 7-8 minutes, remove cover and increase heat to lightly brown onions. Stir in flour, purée, paprika, cayenne and mace, gradually stir in wine and water, bring to the boil and simmer, lid off, for 30-35 minutes. Season with salt and pepper and set aside.

Meanwhile, wash and dry the fish steaks. Butter an ovenproof casserole dish add the fish steaks, sprinkle with salt, pepper and lemon juice or tarragon vinegar. Cover and cook in a moderate oven for 15–20 minutes. Cut bread slices to size of fish steaks and cook in oil until golden brown on each side, drain on paper towels.

Serve fried bread, topped with fish steaks, and spoon sauce over.

# Indian Fish

Serves:   4
Cooking time:   50–55 minutes
Oven:   150°C   300°F

> 1½ lbs (750 g) cod, skinned, boned and diced
> 2 large potatoes, peeled and diced
> flour
> salt and pepper
> oil for frying
> 4 medium onions, finely chopped
> 1 tablespoon ground ginger
> 1½ tablespoons extra flour
> 2 cups (500 ml) concentrated fish stock — see recipe page 89

Roll fish and potatoes, separately, in flour seasoned with salt and pepper. Heat oil in a deep pan, when hot add fish and cook until golden brown, remove fish and set aside. Add potatoes to hot oil and cook until golden brown, remove and place with the fish.

Place onions in a fine strainer and pour boiling water over to blanch, drain well, then mix with ginger in a bowl and pound to a paste, add 1 tablespoon flour and stir in a little stock, mix until smooth. Gradually add remaining stock, then turn mixture into an ovenproof casserole dish and bring the boil. Add fish and potatoes, cover and cook a slow oven for 40–45 minutes.

# Fried Eel with Ravigote Sauce

Serves:   4–6
Cooking time:   30–35 minutes

> 1½ lbs (750 g) of eel, skinned and washed
> ¼ cup (65 ml) lemon juice
> 3 tablespoons flour
> salt and pepper
> ½ cup (125 ml) milk
> 1 egg, beaten
> oil for frying
> parsley
> lemon wedges

**Ravigote Sauce:**
> ¼ cup (65 ml) white wine
> ¼ cup (65 ml) vinegar
> 4 scallions, finely chopped
> 1 cup (250 ml) scalded heavy cream
> 3 tablespoons butter
> dash of chervil
> dash of tarragon
> dash of chives

Cut the eel into 4″ (10 cm) pieces and fillet. Place in a bowl and add lemon juice, let stand to marinate for 1 hour, stirring occasionally.

Mix flour, salt and pepper with a little milk until smooth, gradually stir in remaining milk and fold in egg, stir until smooth for batter.

Heat oil in a deep pan. Drain eel pieces and dry. Dip in batter and cook in hot oil until crisp and brown. Remove with a slotted spoon and drain well on paper towels, place on a platter and keep warm.

To make ravigote sauce: combine wine, vinegar and scallions in a pan and bring to the boil and cook briskly to reduce liquid to ¼ cup (65 ml). Add cream and simmer gently for 5–6 minutes. Remove pan from heat, add butter, chervil, tarragon and chives, then heat.

Serve fried eel garnished with parsley and lemon wedges with ravigote sauce on the side.

# Herring Pie

Serves: 4
Cooking time: 50–55 minutes
Oven: 180°C 350°F

4 herrings, boned and cut into cubes
salted water
4 medium potatoes, peeled
3 tablespoons butter
2 cooking apples, chopped
3 scallions, chopped
salt and pepper
¼ cup (65 ml) fish stock or water
½ cup (125 ml) white wine

Soak fish in salted water for 10 minutes, drain well and set aside. Place potatoes in boiling water for 5 minutes, remove, dry and slice thinly. Brush an ovenproof casserole dish with half the butter, melted, then line the dish thickly with potato slices. Place a layer of herrings in the dish, season with salt and pepper and cover with a layer of apple and scallions, repeat until dish is full. Finish with a layer of potato slices. Combine fish stock or water and wine and pour over the potato and fish mixture. Cover and cook in a moderate oven for 35 minutes. Remove cover, dot top with remaining butter and cook a further 15–20 minutes, until top is golden brown.

# Gefillte Fish

Serves: 4–6
Cooking time: 1¼ hours

½ lb (250 g) snapper fillets
½ lb (250 g) bream fillets
½ lb (250 g) flathead fillets
½ lb (250 g) cod or mullet fillets
2 cups (500 ml) concentrated fish stock — see recipe page 89
1 medium onion, minced
1 medium carrot, grated
2 eggs
salt and pepper
1 teaspoon ground ginger
2 tablespoons cracker crumbs

Pour stock into a flameproof casserole and bring to the boil, reduce heat and simmer.
Meanwhile, mince or finely chop all the fish and combine with onion, carrot, eggs, salt, pepper, ginger and cracker crumbs and mix well. With wet hands shape the mixture into balls and add to the simmering stock. Cover and simmer for 1 hour. Carefully remove balls with a slotted spoon to a deep dish and keep warm. Boil stock briskly to reduce to 1 cup, then strain stock over the balls. Serve piping hot or chill and serve cold.

# Court-Bouillon for Fish

1 small onion stuck with 3 cloves
4 peppercorns
1 bay leaf
top leaves of 1 celery stalk
1 slice of lemon
1 teaspoon salt
2 cups (500 ml) water

Combine all ingredients in a pan, bring to the boil, cover and simmer for 20 minutes. Strain off liquid and reserve for use.

# Wine Court-Bouillon for Fish

1 medium onion, sliced
1 medium carrot, sliced
6 peppercorns
2 cloves
1 bay leaf
top leaves of 2 celery stalks
3 sprigs of parsley
1 teaspoon thyme
1¼ cups (300 ml) dry white wine
1¼ cups (300 ml) water

Combine all ingredients in a pan, bring to the boil, cover and simmer for 30 minutes. Strain off liquid and reserve for use.

# Concentrated Fish Stock

1 lb (500 g) fish bones and trimmings, chopped
1½ tablespoons butter
1 small onion, finely chopped
2 sprigs parsley
4 peppercorns
1 cup (250 ml) water
1 cup (250 ml) white wine
pinch salt

Melt butter in a pan, add fish bones and trimmings, onion, parsley and peppercorns, cover and simmer for 7–8 minutes. Stir in water and wine, cover and simmer for 30 minutes. Strain through muslin. Liquid will keep for a few days refrigerated.

# Easy Cream Mustard Sauce

1 teaspoon prepared hot mustard
salt and pepper
2–3 drops of lemon juice
½ cup (125 ml) thick cream, whipped

Mix mustard, salt, pepper and lemon juice together and add whipped cream a little at a time, stirring briskly until combined. For cold dishes.

# Mornay Sauce

3 tablespoons butter
3 tablespoons flour
1¼ cups (300 ml) milk
3 tablespoons grated cheese

Melt butter in a pan, stir in flour and cook, stirring, until bubbly, gradually stir in milk and bring to the boil, stirring constantly, until thick and smooth. Fold in cheese and, still stirring, simmer 2–3 minutes.

# Onion Sauce

1½ tablespoons butter
3 tablespoons sugar
2 medium onions, chopped
1 cup (250 ml) concentrated fish stock — see recipe this page
1 tablespoon wine vinegar
pinch of salt

Melt butter in a pan, add sugar and caramelize lightly over heat, add onion and sauté until soft. Stir in fish stock, wine vinegar and salt and bring to the boil. Reduce heat, cover and simmer gently for 20–25 minutes.

# Lemon Butter Sauce

3 tablespoons butter
1½ tablespoon cornstarch
¼ cup (65 ml) water
1 egg yolk
¼ cup (65 ml) lemon juice

Melt butter in a pan, stir in cornstarch and mix until smooth, stir in water and bring to the boil, stirring constantly, until sauce starts to thicken, remove from heat. Beat egg yolk, add a little of the sauce and beat. Fold egg and lemon juice into the sauce and heat, but do not boil.

# Tarragon Sauce

1½ tablespoons butter
1½ tablespoons flour
¾ cup (185 ml) concentrated fish stock — see recipe this page
salt and pepper
2 teaspoons tarragon
1 egg, beaten

Melt butter in a pan, add flour and cook, stirring, until bubbly, stir in stock and cook, stirring constantly, until mixture is thick and smooth. Stir in salt, pepper and tarragon and fold in egg, heat, but do not boil. Serve at once.

# Anchovy Sauce

*3 tablespoons butter*
*1 teaspoon anchovy paste*
*1 tablespoon capers, chopped*
*1 tablespoon sherry*
*1 teaspoon lemon juice*
*1 teaspoon chervil*
*salt and pepper*

Melt butter in a pan, stir in anchovy paste and capers and sauté 2–3 minutes. Stir in sherry, lemon juice, chervil, salt and pepper and simmer, stirring, for 5–6 minutes.

# Hollandaise Sauce

*3 tablespoons wine vinegar*
*4 peppercorns, bruised*
*1 bay leaf*
*1 egg yolk*
*4 tablespoons softened butter*
*pinch of salt*
*few drops of lemon juice*

Combine vinegar, peppercorns and bay leaf in a pan and simmer until liquid is reduced by half, then strain liquid and reserve.
Beat egg yolk with a little butter and salt in top of a double pan over heat and cook, stirring with a wooden spoon, until creamed. Stir in reserved liquid, gradually add butter, stirring constantly; then add lemon juice and cook, stirring, until thick and smooth.

# Quick Hollandaise Sauce

*3 egg yolks*
*2 tablespoons lemon juice*
*1½ tablespoons hot water*
*¾ cup (185 g) butter, melted*
*1 teaspoon prepared mustard*
*½ teaspoon salt*
*1 tablespoon chopped parsley*
*1 tablespoon chopped chives*

In a blender combine egg yolks and lemon juice and blend 1–2 minutes, add hot water, then on high speed pour in melted butter in a steady stream, blend for 2 minutes, add mustard and salt and blend 1 minute. Turn sauce into a bowl and stir in parsley and chives and mix well. Makes about 1½ cups.

# Parsley Sauce for Fish

*1½ tablespoons butter*
*1½ tablespoons flour*
*½ cup (125 ml) concentrated fish stock — see recipe page 89*
*salt and pepper*
*2 tablespoons chopped parsley*
*¼ cup (65 ml) cream*
*1 egg, beaten*

Melt butter in a pan, add flour and cook until bubbly, stir in stock and cook, stirring constantly, until mixture starts to thicken. Remove from heat and stir in salt, pepper, parsley and cream. Return to heat and simmer gently 2–3 minutes, do not boil. Fold in egg and serve at once.

# Hot Tartare Sauce

*1 tablespoon butter*
*1 small onion, minced*
*1 tablespoon cornstarch*
*1 cup (250 ml) milk*
*2 tablespoons mayonnaise*
*2 teaspoons minced capers*
*1 tablespoon chopped parsley*
*salt and pepper*

Melt butter in a pan, add onion and sauté until soft, remove from heat and stir in cornstarch until smooth, gradually stir in milk, return to heat and bring to the boil, stirring constantly and simmer until thick and smooth. Fold in mayonnaise, capers, parsley, salt and pepper and heat. Serve hot.

# Tartare Sauce — cold

*½ cup mayonnaise*
*1 tablespoon chopped capers*
*1 tablespoon chopped gherkins*
*½ teaspoon chopped chives*
*2 teaspoons chopped parsley*

In a bowl combine all ingredients and mix thoroughly and chill.

# Caper Butter Sauce

*4 tablespoons butter*
*3 tablespoons chopped capers*
*pinch of salt*
*2 teaspoons lemon juice*

Melt butter in a pan, stir in capers and salt and simmer 2–3 minutes, stir in lemon juice and serve at once over fish.

# Garlic Butter

Whip 2 tablespoons of softened butter to a cream and blend with 1 crushed clove of garlic. Spoon onto a plastic sheet or waxed paper and roll into a sausage shape. Chill and cut in slices for pats of garlic butter.

# Mustard Butter

Mix 1 teaspoon of dry mustard and a pinch of salt with ½ teaspoon of white wine or water until smooth and blend with 4 tablespoons of softened butter. Spoon onto a plastic sheet of waxed paper and roll into a sausage shape. Chill and cut in slices for pats of mustard butter.

# Savoury Butter

Cream 4 tablespoons of softened butter until lemon coloured and light and blend with 1 teaspoon dry mustard, 4 teaspoons Worcestershire sauce, ½ teaspoon Tabasco sauce, 2 teaspoons of minced onion and 2 teaspoons of finely chopped parsley and beat until fluffy.

# Green Butter

Steam 3 spinach leaves, 1 scallion, 1 sprig parsley and ½ teaspoon tarragon with ¼ cup (65 ml) of water, covered, for 5 minutes. Cool and strain off liquid and discard. Rub through a sieve and blend with 6 tablespoons of softened butter. Spoon onto a plastic sheet or waxed paper and roll into a sausage shape. Chill and cut in slices for pats of green butter.

# Maitre d'Hotel Butter

Cream 6 tablespoons of butter until light and lemon coloured and blend with 1 teaspoon finely chopped parsley, 2 teaspoons lemon juice, salt and pepper and beat until frothy.

# Whipped Butter for Fish

Combine ½ cup Maitre d'Hotel Butter with ½ teaspoon tarragon and 2 teaspoons concentrated fish stock (see recipe page 89) and whip to a froth.

# Scallion Butter

Steam 3 finely chopped scallions and ½ teaspoon finely chopped chives in a covered pan, with 2 teaspoons of water or white wine for 2–3 minutes. Drain thoroughly and put through a sieve. Blend with 4 tablespoons softened butter, using the flat of a knife or a spatula. Spoon onto a plastic sheet or waxed paper and roll into a sausage shape. Chill and cut in slices for pats of scallion butter.

# Parsley Butter

Blend 4 tablespoons softened butter with 1 tablespoon of finely chopped parsley, using the flat of a knife or a spatula. Spoon onto plastic sheet or waxed paper and roll into a sausage shape. Chill and cut in slices for pats of parsley butter.

# Mixed Herb Butter

Blend 3 tablespoons of softened butter with ½ teaspoon each of finely chopped parsley, tarragon, chives, scallions and chervil, using the flat of a knife or a spatula. Spoon onto a plastic sheet or waxed paper and roll into a sausage shape. Chill and cut in slices for pats of mixed herb butter.

# Tarragon Butter

Blend 3 tablespoons of softened butter with 1 teaspoon of tarragon, using the flat of a knife or a spatula. Spoon onto a plastic sheet or waxed paper and roll into a sausage shape. Chill and cut in slices for pats of tarragon butter.

# Anchovy Butter

Blend 4 tablespoons of softened butter with 1 tablespoon of anchovy paste or pounded anchovy fillet, using the flat of a knife or a spatula. Spoon onto a plastic sheet or waxed paper and roll into a sausage shape. Chill and cut in slices for pats of anchovy butter.

# Shrimp Butter

Mince 3 cooked fresh shrimp, shelled and deveined, and blend with 3 tablespoons softened butter, using the flat of a knife or a spatula. Spoon onto plastic sheet or waxed paper and roll into a sausage shape. Chill and cut in slices for pats of shrimp butter.

# Liquid Measures Table

| IMPERIAL | METRIC |
|---|---|
| 1 teaspoon | 5 ml |
| *1 tablespoon (Aust) | 20 ml |
| 2 fluid ounces (¼ cup) | 65 ml |
| 4 fluid ounces (½ cup) | 125 ml |
| 8 fluid ounces (1 cup) | 250 ml |
| 1 pint (20 fluid ounces = 2½ cups) | 625 ml |

| USA | METRIC |
|---|---|
| *1 tablespoon (also UK and NZ) | 15 ml |
| 1 pint (16 ounces = 2 cups) | 500 ml |
| All other measures same as for imperial, above | |

*Tablespoon measures used in the recipes in this book are 15 ml.

# Solid Measures Table

| AVOIRDUPOIS | METRIC |
|---|---|
| 1 ounce | 30 g |
| 4 ounces (¼ lb) | 125 g |
| 8 ounces (½ lb) | 250 g |
| 12 ounces (¾ lb) | 375 g |
| 16 ounces (1 lb) | 500 g |
| 24 ounces (1½ lb) | 750 g |
| 32 ounces (2 lb) | 1000 g (1 kg) |

# Oven Temperature Table

| DESCRIPTION | GAS | | ELECTRIC | | DIAL MARK |
|---|---|---|---|---|---|
| | C | F | C | F | |
| Cool | 100 | 200 | 110 | 225 | ¼ |
| Very slow | 120 | 250 | 120 | 250 | ½ |
| Slow | 150 | 300 | 150 | 300 | 1–2 |
| Moderately slow | 160 | 325 | 170 | 340 | 3 |
| Moderate | 180 | 350 | 190 | 375 | 4 |
| Moderately hot | 190 | 375 | 220 | 425 | 5–6 |
| Hot | 200 | 400 | 250 | 475 | 6–7 |
| Very hot | 230 | 450 | 270 | 525 | 8–9 |

# Index

# Notes

Salmon Steaks
  1 C burgandy
  1/4 C water
  2 Tbl. soy sauce

Marinate 4 hrs. - broil skin side
down - brush w/ butter